CB 16-35 | BEA 16-12 | FT-900 (16-01)

U.S. Census Bureau
U.S. Bureau of Economic Analysis
NEWS

U.S. Department of Commerce • Washington, DC 20230

FOR IMMEDIATE RELEASE AT 8:30 A.M. EST, FRIDAY, MARCH 4, 2016

For information on goods contact:
U.S. Census Bureau
Matthew Przybocki 301-763-2311

For information on services contact:
U.S. Bureau of Economic Analysis
Technical: Jeffrey Bogen 202-606-9592
Media: Jeannine Aversa 202-606-2649

U.S. INTERNATIONAL TRADE IN GOODS AND SERVICES
January 2016

The U.S. Census Bureau and the U.S. Bureau of Economic Analysis, through the Department of Commerce, announced today that the goods and services deficit was **$45.7 billion** in January, up $1.0 billion from $44.7 billion in December, revised. January exports were **$176.5 billion**, $3.8 billion less than December exports. January imports were **$222.1 billion**, $2.8 billion less than December imports.

The January increase in the goods and services deficit reflected an increase in the goods deficit of $1.1 billion to $63.7 billion and an increase in the services surplus of $0.1 billion to $18.0 billion.

Year-over-year, the goods and services deficit increased $2.1 billion, or 4.8 percent, from January 2015. Exports decreased $12.5 billion or 6.6 percent. Imports decreased $10.5 billion or 4.5 percent.

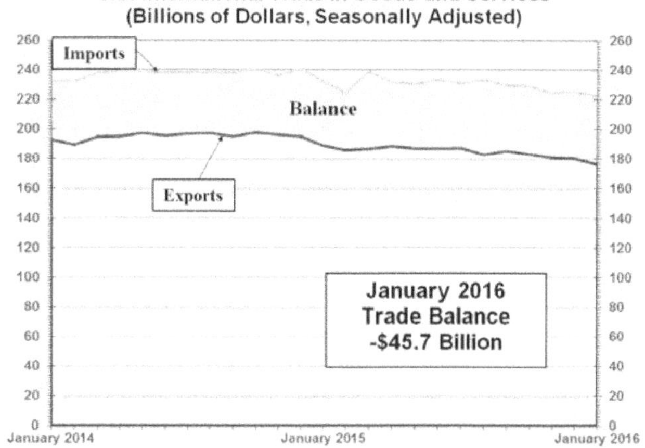

Goods and Services Three-Month Moving Averages (Exhibit 2)

The average goods and services deficit increased $0.1 billion to $44.6 billion for the three months ending in January.

- Average exports of goods and services decreased $2.2 billion to $179.2 billion in January.
- Average imports of goods and services decreased $2.2 billion to $223.9 billion in January.

Year-over-year, the average goods and services deficit increased $1.6 billion from the three months ending in January 2015.

- Average exports of goods and services decreased $14.2 billion from January 2015.
- Average imports of goods and services decreased $12.6 billion from January 2015.

NOTE: All statistics referenced are seasonally adjusted; statistics are on a balance of payments basis unless otherwise specified. Additional statistics, including not seasonally adjusted statistics and details for goods on a Census basis, are available in Exhibits 1-20b of this release. For information on data sources, definitions, revision procedures, and scheduled release dates through December 2016, see the information section on page A-1 of this release. The next release is **April 5, 2016.**

Exports (Exhibits 3, 6, and 7)

Exports of goods decreased $4.0 billion to $116.9 billion in January.

Exports of goods on a Census basis decreased $3.9 billion.

- Capital goods decreased $1.2 billion.
- Industrial supplies and materials decreased $0.9 billion.
  - Fuel oil decreased $0.7 billion.
- Consumer goods decreased $0.8 billion.

Net balance of payments adjustments decreased $0.1 billion.

Exports of services increased $0.2 billion to $59.6 billion in January.

- Travel (for all purposes including education) increased $0.2 billion.
- Transport, which includes freight and port services and passenger fares, increased $0.1 billion.

Imports (Exhibits 4, 6, and 8)

Imports of goods decreased $2.9 billion to $180.6 billion in January.

Imports of goods on a Census basis decreased $2.8 billion.

- Industrial supplies and materials decreased $2.1 billion.
  - Crude oil decreased $1.8 billion.
- Capital goods decreased $1.2 billion.
  - Civilian aircraft decreased $0.9 billion.

Net balance of payments adjustments decreased $0.1 billion.

Imports of services increased less than $0.1 billion to $41.5 billion in January.

- Other business services, which includes research and development services; professional and management services; and technical, trade-related, and other services, increased $0.1 billion.
- Travel (for all purposes including education) increased $0.1 billion.

Real Goods in 2009 Dollars – Census Basis (Exhibit 11)

The real goods deficit increased $1.9 billion to $62.0 billion in January.

- Real exports of goods decreased $2.6 billion to $116.0 billion.
- Real imports of goods decreased $0.7 billion to $178.0 billion.

Revisions

Exports and imports of goods and services were revised for July through December 2015 to incorporate more comprehensive and updated quarterly and monthly data. In addition to these revisions, seasonally adjusted data for all months in 2015 were revised so that the totals of the seasonally adjusted months equal the annual totals.

Revisions to December exports

- Exports of goods were revised downward $0.3 billion.
- Exports of services were revised downward $1.0 billion.

Revisions to December imports

- Imports of goods were revised downward $0.2 billion.
- Imports of services were revised upward $0.3 billion.

Goods by Selected Countries and Areas: Monthly – Census Basis (Exhibit 19)

The January figures show surpluses, in billions of dollars, with South and Central America ($3.1) and Brazil ($0.6). Deficits were recorded, in billions of dollars, with China ($31.1), European Union ($12.6), Germany ($5.8), Japan ($5.6), Mexico ($5.6), South Korea ($2.9), Italy ($2.4), India ($2.3), France ($1.5), Canada ($0.5), Saudi Arabia ($0.2), OPEC ($0.2), and United Kingdom ($0.1).

- The deficit with **China** increased $1.4 billion to $31.1 billion in January. Exports increased less than $0.1 billion to $8.6 billion and imports increased $1.5 billion to $39.8 billion.
- The deficit with **Mexico** increased $0.8 billion to $5.6 billion in January. Exports decreased less than $0.1 billion to $19.5 billion and imports increased $0.8 billion to $25.1 billion.

Goods and Services by Selected Countries and Areas: Quarterly – Balance of Payments Basis (Exhibit 20)

The fourth quarter figures show surpluses, in billions of dollars, with South and Central America ($13.9), OPEC ($7.7), Brazil ($4.8), United Kingdom ($4.1), Canada ($2.5), and Saudi Arabia ($2.2). Deficits were recorded, in billions of dollars, with China ($83.0), European Union ($29.0), Germany ($19.1), Mexico ($16.5), Japan ($14.7), Italy ($8.2), India ($7.9), France ($4.5), and South Korea ($3.6).

- The balance with **Canada** shifted from a deficit of $1.0 billion to a surplus of $2.5 billion in the fourth quarter. Exports decreased $1.6 billion to $82.3 billion and imports decreased $5.1 billion to $79.8 billion.
- The surplus with the **United Kingdom** increased $2.5 billion to $4.1 billion in the fourth quarter. Exports increased $0.6 billion to $30.2 billion and imports decreased $1.9 billion to $26.1 billion.

NOTE: For definitions of goods on a balance of payments basis, goods on a Census basis, and net balance of payments adjustments, see the information section on page A-1 of this release.

NOTICE

With this release of the "U.S. International Trade in Goods and Services" report (FT-900) and the accompanying FT-900 Supplement, the following changes have been made:

Changes to Exhibits 7, 8, and 17a of the FT-900

Commodity detail is now presented for the end-use category *Automotive vehicles, parts, and engines* in Exhibits 7 and 8.

The following countries have been removed from Exhibit 17a because of consistently low crude oil imports: Bolivia, Congo (Kinshasa), Ghana, Guatemala, Kazakhstan, Oman, Peru, Thailand, Trinidad and Tobago, Vietnam, and Yemen.

Change to OPEC

OPEC now includes Indonesia, which rejoined on January 1, 2016. This change affects Exhibits 14, 17a, and 19 of the FT-900 and Exhibit 4 of the FT-900 Supplement. This change will also affect Exhibits 20, 20a, and 20b of the FT-900 with the April 2016 release on June 3, 2016.

If you have questions or need additional information, please contact the U.S. Census Bureau, Economic Indicators Division, on (800) 549-0595, option 4, or at eid.international.trade.data@census.gov.

To learn more about the FT-900 and other economic indicators the Census Bureau publishes, join the Economic Indicators Division for the "Investigating Economic Indicators" Webinar series. For more information, visit www.census.gov/econ/webinar.

Table of Contents

Part A: Seasonally Adjusted (by Commodity/Service)

Exhibit 1. U.S. International Trade in Goods and Services

In millions of dollars. Details may not equal totals due to seasonal adjustment and rounding. (R) - Revised.

Period	Balance			Exports			Imports		
	Total	Goods (1)	Services	Total	Goods (1)	Services	Total	Goods (1)	Services
2014									
Jan. - Dec.	-508,324	-741,462	233,138	2,343,205	1,632,639	710,565	2,851,529	2,374,101	477,428
Jan. -	-39,462	-59,968	20,506	192,879	133,738	59,141	232,341	193,706	38,635
January	-39,462	-59,968	20,506	192,879	133,738	59,141	232,341	193,706	38,635
February	-42,835	-61,292	18,457	189,495	131,768	57,726	232,330	193,060	39,270
March	-43,121	-63,050	19,929	194,759	135,923	58,837	237,881	198,973	38,908
April	-44,271	-64,321	20,051	195,024	135,556	59,468	239,295	199,877	39,417
May	-42,070	-62,091	20,021	197,269	137,314	59,955	239,340	199,405	39,934
June	-42,371	-61,700	19,330	195,579	136,282	59,298	237,950	197,982	39,968
July	-41,411	-60,177	18,767	196,907	138,406	58,500	238,317	198,584	39,734
August	-41,275	-60,824	19,549	197,303	138,155	59,148	238,578	198,979	39,599
September	-43,186	-62,075	18,889	195,053	136,371	58,682	238,239	198,446	39,793
October	-42,753	-61,917	19,163	197,759	138,107	59,652	240,513	200,024	40,489
November	-40,021	-59,331	19,309	196,201	136,474	59,726	236,222	195,805	40,417
December	-45,549	-64,716	19,167	194,975	134,544	60,431	240,524	199,260	41,264
2015									
Jan. - Dec. (R)	-539,755	-759,307	219,552	2,223,618	1,513,453	710,165	2,763,374	2,272,760	490,613
Jan. - (R)	-43,601	-62,978	19,377	189,000	129,266	59,735	232,602	192,244	40,357
January (R)	-43,601	-62,978	19,377	189,000	129,266	59,735	232,602	192,244	40,357
February (R)	-38,550	-58,069	19,518	185,865	126,303	59,561	224,415	184,372	40,043
March (R)	-52,176	-71,192	19,016	186,741	127,157	59,584	238,917	198,349	40,567
April (R)	-43,379	-62,027	18,647	188,407	129,320	59,086	231,786	191,347	40,439
May (R)	-43,457	-62,105	18,648	187,065	127,808	59,257	230,522	189,913	40,609
June (R)	-46,271	-65,143	18,872	186,905	127,499	59,406	233,177	192,642	40,534
July (R)	-43,710	-61,475	17,765	187,199	128,503	58,696	230,909	189,978	40,931
August (R)	-50,544	-67,884	17,340	182,810	124,246	58,564	233,353	192,129	41,224
September (R)	-44,321	-61,153	16,831	185,289	126,697	58,593	229,611	187,849	41,761
October (R)	-45,476	-63,189	17,713	183,149	124,037	59,113	228,625	187,225	41,400
November (R)	-43,571	-61,492	17,921	180,903	121,717	59,186	224,474	183,209	41,265
December (R)	-44,698	-62,600	17,902	180,284	120,900	59,384	224,983	183,501	41,482
2016									
Jan. -	-45,677	-63,718	18,041	176,456	116,890	59,565	222,133	180,609	41,524
January	-45,677	-63,718	18,041	176,456	116,890	59,565	222,133	180,609	41,524
February									
March									
April									
May									
June									
July									
August									
September									
October									
November									
December									
December data as published last month:	-43,357	-62,514	19,157	181,497	121,155	60,343	224,854	183,669	41,185

(1) Data are presented on a balance of payments (BOP) basis.

NOTE: For information on data sources and methodology, see the information section on page A-1 of this release or at www.census.gov/ft900 or www.bea.gov/newsreleases/international/trade/tradnewsrelease.htm.

Part A: Seasonally Adjusted (by Commodity/Service)

Exhibit 2. U.S. International Trade in Goods and Services
Three-Month Moving Averages

In millions of dollars. Details may not equal totals due to seasonal adjustment and rounding. (R) - Revised.

Month of Moving Average	Balance			Exports			Imports		
	Total	Goods (1)	Services	Total	Goods (1)	Services	Total	Goods (1)	Services
2014									
January	-37,558	-57,088	19,530	193,640	134,953	58,687	231,198	192,041	39,157
February	-39,915	-59,345	19,429	191,784	133,281	58,503	231,699	192,626	39,074
March	-41,806	-61,437	19,631	192,378	133,810	58,568	234,184	195,246	38,937
April	-43,409	-62,888	19,479	193,093	134,416	58,677	236,502	197,303	39,198
May	-43,154	-63,154	20,000	195,684	136,264	59,420	238,838	199,419	39,420
June	-42,904	-62,704	19,800	195,958	136,384	59,574	238,862	199,088	39,773
July	-41,951	-61,323	19,372	196,585	137,334	59,251	238,536	198,657	39,879
August	-41,685	-60,901	19,215	196,597	137,614	58,982	238,282	198,515	39,767
September	-41,957	-61,025	19,068	196,421	137,644	58,777	238,378	198,670	39,709
October	-42,405	-61,605	19,200	196,705	137,545	59,161	239,110	199,150	39,960
November	-41,987	-61,107	19,121	196,338	136,984	59,353	238,324	198,092	40,233
December	-42,774	-61,988	19,213	196,312	136,375	59,937	239,086	198,363	40,723
2015									
January (R)	-43,057	-62,342	19,285	193,392	133,428	59,964	236,449	195,770	40,679
February (R)	-42,567	-61,921	19,354	189,947	130,038	59,909	232,513	191,959	40,555
March (R)	-44,776	-64,080	19,304	187,202	127,575	59,627	231,978	191,655	40,323
April (R)	-44,702	-63,763	19,061	187,004	127,594	59,410	231,706	191,356	40,350
May (R)	-46,337	-65,108	18,771	187,404	128,095	59,309	233,741	193,203	40,538
June (R)	-44,369	-63,092	18,722	187,459	128,209	59,250	231,828	191,301	40,527
July (R)	-44,479	-62,908	18,428	187,057	127,937	59,120	231,536	190,845	40,691
August (R)	-46,842	-64,834	17,992	185,638	126,749	58,889	232,480	191,583	40,897
September (R)	-46,192	-63,504	17,312	185,099	126,482	58,618	231,291	189,986	41,306
October (R)	-46,780	-64,075	17,295	183,750	124,993	58,757	230,530	189,068	41,462
November (R)	-44,456	-61,945	17,488	183,114	124,150	58,964	227,570	186,095	41,475
December (R)	-44,582	-62,427	17,845	181,446	122,218	59,228	226,027	184,645	41,382
2016									
January	-44,649	-62,604	17,955	179,214	119,836	59,378	223,863	182,440	41,424
February									
March									
April									
May									
June									
July									
August									
September									
October									
November									
December									

(1) Data are presented on a BOP basis.

NOTES:

* The three-month moving averages shown in this exhibit are computed by summing the subject month and the two prior months, dividing by three, and showing the average at the end month of the period. A moving average is useful in smoothing the volatile trade data so that trends can better be discerned.
* For information on data sources and methodology, see the information section on page A-1 of this release or at www.census.gov/ft900 or www.bea.gov/newsreleases/international/trade/tradnewsrelease.htm.

Part A: Seasonally Adjusted (by Commodity/Service)

Exhibit 3. U.S. Exports of Services by Major Category

In millions of dollars. Details may not equal totals due to seasonal adjustment and rounding. (R) - Revised.

Period	Total Services	Maintenance and Repair Services n.i.e.	Transport	Travel (for all purposes including education) (1)	Insurance Services	Financial Services	Charges for the Use of Intellectual Property n.i.e.	Telecommuni-cations, Computer, and Information Services	Other Business Services	Government Goods and Services n.i.e.
2014										
Jan. - Dec.	710,565	22,389	90,031	177,241	17,417	87,290	130,362	35,885	129,514	20,438
Jan. -	59,141	1,646	7,533	15,232	1,408	7,060	10,806	2,924	10,562	1,970
January	59,141	1,646	7,533	15,232	1,408	7,060	10,806	2,924	10,562	1,970
February	57,726	1,632	7,118	14,232	1,388	6,924	10,882	2,923	10,645	1,983
March	58,837	1,726	7,431	14,726	1,405	7,088	10,940	2,960	10,652	1,910
April	59,468	1,810	7,473	14,919	1,458	7,478	10,982	3,035	10,582	1,731
May	59,955	1,883	7,674	15,158	1,483	7,520	10,976	3,070	10,549	1,643
June	59,298	1,898	7,427	14,852	1,481	7,458	10,923	3,065	10,554	1,638
July	58,500	1,869	7,421	14,418	1,452	7,184	10,822	3,019	10,597	1,717
August	59,148	1,911	7,695	14,869	1,441	7,043	10,769	2,988	10,706	1,725
September	58,682	1,890	7,505	14,435	1,447	7,124	10,764	2,973	10,880	1,664
October	59,652	1,985	7,510	14,673	1,471	7,559	10,805	2,974	11,120	1,554
November	59,726	2,041	7,457	14,837	1,487	7,336	10,836	2,975	11,287	1,469
December	60,431	2,097	7,787	14,889	1,495	7,515	10,858	2,978	11,380	1,433
2015										
Jan. - Dec. (R)	710,165	24,123	84,225	178,297	18,665	86,286	126,210	36,989	135,260	20,110
Jan. - (R)	59,735	1,806	7,317	14,898	1,506	7,534	10,631	3,055	11,389	1,599
January (R)	59,735	1,806	7,317	14,898	1,506	7,534	10,631	3,055	11,389	1,599
February (R)	59,561	1,717	7,190	14,823	1,512	7,537	10,551	3,100	11,434	1,697
March (R)	59,584	1,704	7,165	14,645	1,519	7,656	10,541	3,114	11,514	1,727
April (R)	59,086	1,850	7,013	14,644	1,526	7,284	10,581	3,122	11,391	1,675
May (R)	59,257	1,929	7,055	14,920	1,531	7,072	10,601	3,134	11,349	1,666
June (R)	59,406	1,994	6,959	14,947	1,534	7,161	10,594	3,150	11,387	1,680
July (R)	58,696	2,025	6,895	14,820	1,573	6,906	10,535	3,074	11,108	1,761
August (R)	58,564	2,073	6,926	14,805	1,590	6,872	10,492	3,031	10,977	1,799
September (R)	58,593	2,109	6,841	14,934	1,597	6,852	10,457	3,023	10,991	1,790
October (R)	59,113	2,244	7,028	14,975	1,594	7,086	10,430	3,048	11,152	1,556
November (R)	59,186	2,319	6,918	14,960	1,592	7,094	10,408	3,065	11,259	1,572
December (R)	59,384	2,353	6,918	14,926	1,591	7,233	10,390	3,075	11,310	1,589
2016										
Jan. -	59,565	2,200	7,038	15,097	1,591	7,266	10,376	3,075	11,307	1,615
January	59,565	2,200	7,038	15,097	1,591	7,266	10,376	3,075	11,307	1,615
February										
March										
April										
May										
June										
July										
August										
September										
October										
November										
December										
December data as published last month:	60,343	2,061	6,970	14,942	1,546	7,713	10,432	3,234	11,909	1,536

n.i.e. Not included elsewhere

(1) All travel purposes include 1) business travel, including expenditures by border, seasonal, and other short-term workers and 2) personal travel, including health-related and education-related travel.

NOTE: For information on data sources, methodology, and definitions, see the information section on page A-1 of this release or at www.census.gov/ft900 or www.bea.gov/newsreleases/international/trade/tradnewsrelease.htm.

Part A: Seasonally Adjusted (by Commodity/Service)

Exhibit 4. U.S. Imports of Services by Major Category

In millions of dollars. Details may not equal totals due to seasonal adjustment and rounding. (R) - Revised.

Period	Total Services	Maintenance and Repair Services n.i.e.	Transport	Travel (for all purposes including education) (1)	Insurance Services	Financial Services	Charges for the Use of Intellectual Property n.i.e.	Telecommuni-cations, Computer, and Information Services	Other Business Services	Government Goods and Services n.i.e.
2014										
Jan. - Dec.	477,428	7,468	94,219	110,787	50,096	19,503	42,124	33,314	95,752	24,163
Jan. -	38,635	568	7,623	8,706	4,154	1,574	3,277	2,783	7,933	2,018
January	38,635	568	7,623	8,706	4,154	1,574	3,277	2,783	7,933	2,018
February	39,270	587	7,642	8,742	4,107	1,510	3,987	2,781	7,903	2,010
March	38,908	607	7,827	8,860	4,119	1,562	3,232	2,777	7,912	2,012
April	39,417	627	7,783	9,127	4,189	1,602	3,336	2,770	7,958	2,025
May	39,934	627	7,877	9,396	4,222	1,638	3,411	2,768	7,959	2,035
June	39,968	623	7,756	9,377	4,217	1,673	3,589	2,774	7,917	2,043
July	39,734	625	7,725	9,320	4,174	1,663	3,562	2,785	7,831	2,048
August	39,599	606	7,783	9,246	4,157	1,652	3,491	2,789	7,833	2,041
September	39,793	623	7,869	9,200	4,165	1,688	3,518	2,785	7,924	2,021
October	40,489	636	7,992	9,567	4,198	1,680	3,550	2,773	8,103	1,990
November	40,417	657	7,947	9,455	4,206	1,628	3,576	2,766	8,216	1,967
December	41,264	681	8,395	9,792	4,188	1,634	3,595	2,763	8,262	1,953
2015										
Jan. - Dec. (R)	490,613	9,251	96,893	120,471	48,331	20,134	39,157	33,155	101,716	21,505
Jan. - (R)	40 357	684	8 092	9 708	4 103	1 584	3 282	2 736	8 300	1 867
January (R)	40,357	684	8,092	9,708	4,103	1,584	3,282	2,736	8,300	1,867
February (R)	40,043	689	8,061	9,663	4,058	1,542	3,168	2,720	8,328	1,813
March (R)	40,567	711	8,507	9,709	4,040	1,599	3,144	2,716	8,350	1,791
April (R)	40,439	704	8,054	9,829	4,048	1,658	3,276	2,732	8,328	1,810
May (R)	40,609	694	8,100	9,870	4,043	1,671	3,343	2,738	8,331	1,818
June (R)	40,534	730	7,900	9,901	4,025	1,704	3,367	2,735	8,356	1,816
July (R)	40,931	791	7,959	10,014	4,067	1,719	3,293	2,781	8,490	1,817
August (R)	41,224	830	8,049	10,131	4,060	1,697	3,259	2,807	8,584	1,806
September (R)	41,761	847	8,132	10,568	4,028	1,708	3,248	2,812	8,633	1,784
October (R)	41,400	852	7,972	10,391	3,971	1,770	3,260	2,795	8,637	1,751
November (R)	41,265	852	8,022	10,257	3,943	1,749	3,262	2,789	8,664	1,725
December (R)	41,482	866	8,043	10,429	3,945	1,732	3,254	2,794	8,714	1,706
2016										
Jan. -	41,524	881	7,950	10,497	3,975	1,696	3,236	2,809	8,787	1,694
January	41,524	881	7,950	10,497	3,975	1,696	3,236	2,809	8,787	1,694
February										
March										
April										
May										
June										
July										
August										
September										
October										
November										
December										
December data as published last month:	41,185	775	8,038	10,415	3,881	1,690	3,336	2,727	8,590	1,734

n.i.e. Not included elsewhere

(1) All travel purposes include 1) business travel, including expenditures by border, seasonal, and other short-term workers and 2) personal travel, including health-related and education-related travel.

NOTE: For information on data sources, methodology, and definitions, see the information section on page A-1 of this release or at www.census.gov/ft900 or www.bea.gov/newsreleases/international/trade/tradnewsrelease.htm.

Part A: Seasonally Adjusted (by Commodity/Service)

Exhibit 5. U.S. Trade in Goods

In millions of dollars. Details may not equal totals due to seasonal adjustment and rounding. (R) - Revised.

Period	Balance		Exports			Imports		
	Total Balance of Payments Basis	Total Census Basis	Total Balance of Payments Basis	Net Adjustments	Total Census Basis	Total Balance of Payments Basis	Net Adjustments	Total Census Basis
2014								
Jan. - Dec.	-741,462	-727,153	1,632,639	12,107	1,620,532	2,374,101	26,416	2,347,685
Jan. -	-59,968	-59,291	133,738	1,630	132,109	193,706	2,306	191,400
January	-59,968	-59,291	133,738	1,630	132,109	193,706	2,306	191,400
February	-61,292	-59,543	131,768	660	131,109	193,060	2,409	190,651
March	-63,050	-61,889	135,923	1,261	134,661	198,973	2,423	196,550
April	-64,321	-63,247	135,556	1,142	134,415	199,877	2,216	197,662
May	-62,091	-61,222	137,314	1,282	136,032	199,405	2,151	197,254
June	-61,700	-60,640	136,282	1,150	135,132	197,982	2,210	195,772
July	-60,177	-59,261	138,406	1,224	137,182	198,584	2,140	196,444
August	-60,824	-59,436	138,155	723	137,433	198,979	2,111	196,869
September	-62,075	-60,638	136,371	691	135,680	198,446	2,127	196,319
October	-61,917	-60,721	138,107	901	137,207	200,024	2,097	197,927
November	-59,331	-58,206	136,474	991	135,483	195,805	2,116	193,689
December	-64,716	-63,058	134,544	453	134,090	199,260	2,111	197,149
2015								
Jan. - Dec. (R)	-759,307	-736,019	1,513,453	8,539	1,504,914	2,272,760	31,828	2,240,933
Jan. - (R)	-62,978	-61,098	129,266	805	128,461	192,244	2,685	189,559
January (R)	-62,978	-61,098	129,266	805	128,461	192,244	2,685	189,559
February (R)	-58,069	-55,968	126,303	714	125,589	184,372	2,815	181,557
March (R)	-71,192	-69,290	127,157	1,043	126,114	198,349	2,946	195,404
April (R)	-62,027	-59,435	129,320	880	128,440	191,347	3,472	187,875
May (R)	-62,105	-59,609	127,808	752	127,056	189,913	3,248	186,665
June (R)	-65,143	-62,350	127,499	907	126,592	192,642	3,700	188,942
July (R)	-61,475	-59,300	128,503	708	127,795	189,978	2,883	187,095
August (R)	-67,884	-66,273	124,246	485	123,760	192,129	2,096	190,034
September (R)	-61,153	-59,465	126,697	285	126,412	187,849	1,973	185,877
October (R)	-63,189	-61,846	124,037	775	123,261	187,225	2,118	185,108
November (R)	-61,492	-60,034	121,717	547	121,169	183,209	2,006	181,203
December (R)	-62,600	-61,351	120,900	637	120,263	183,501	1,886	181,615
2016								
Jan. -	-63,718	-62,398	116,890	504	116,387	180,609	1,824	178,784
January	-63,718	-62,398	116,890	504	116,387	180,609	1,824	178,784
February								
March								
April								
May								
June								
July								
August								
September								
October								
November								
December								
December data as published last month:	-62,514	-61,506	121,155	891	120,264	183,669	1,898	181,770

NOTE: For information on data sources, nonsampling errors, definitions, and details concerning what is included in Net Adjustments, see the information section on page A-1 of this release or at www.census.gov/ft900 or www.bea.gov/newsreleases/international/trade/tradnewsrelease.htm.

Part A: Seasonally Adjusted (by Commodity/Service)

Exhibit 6. U.S. Trade in Goods by Principal End-Use Category

In millions of dollars. Details may not equal totals due to seasonal adjustment and rounding. (R) - Revised.

Period	Total Balance of Payments Basis	Net Adjustments	Total Census Basis (1)	End-Use Commodity Category: Foods, Feeds, & Beverages	Industrial Supplies (2)	Capital Goods	Automotive Vehicles, etc.	Consumer Goods	Other Goods
					Exports				
2015									
Jan. - Dec. (R)	1,513,453	8,539	1,504,914	127,704	428,172	538,341	151,563	197,817	61,317
Jan. - (R)	129,266	805	128,461	11,010	37,573	45,838	12,783	16,760	4,497
January (R)	129,266	805	128,461	11,010	37,573	45,838	12,783	16,760	4,497
February (R)	126,303	714	125,589	10,809	36,265	44,347	11,739	17,765	4,664
March (R)	127,157	1,043	126,114	11,024	36,222	45,220	12,350	16,126	5,171
April (R)	129,320	880	128,440	10,829	36,859	47,298	12,500	16,046	4,910
May (R)	127,808	752	127,056	11,002	37,720	44,847	12,627	15,967	4,895
June (R)	127,499	907	126,592	10,559	37,041	44,082	12,666	16,764	5,480
July (R)	128,503	708	127,795	10,718	37,376	44,289	13,277	16,337	5,798
August (R)	124,246	485	123,760	10,466	35,157	44,390	12,767	15,775	5,205
September (R)	126,697	285	126,412	10,852	35,152	45,300	12,933	17,041	5,134
October (R)	124,037	775	123,261	10,260	33,531	44,363	12,771	16,537	5,799
November (R)	121,717	547	121,169	10,273	32,849	44,352	12,856	15,881	4,959
December (R)	120,900	637	120,263	9,901	32,429	44,015	12,296	16,818	4,804
2016									
Jan. -	116,890	504	116,387	9,429	31,498	42,801	12,315	15,979	4,365
January	116,890	504	116,387	9,429	31,498	42,801	12,315	15,979	4,365
February									
March									
April									
May									
June									
July									
August									
September									
October									
November									
December									
					Imports				
2015									
Jan. - Dec. (R)	2,272,760	31,828	2,240,933	127,689	485,908	599,156	348,283	595,175	84,721
Jan. - (R)	192,244	2,685	189,559	10,673	46,697	50,417	28,110	47,177	6,487
January (R)	192,244	2,685	189,559	10,673	46,697	50,417	28,110	47,177	6,487
February (R)	184,372	2,815	181,557	10,465	42,605	48,678	26,623	46,350	6,836
March (R)	198,349	2,946	195,404	10,957	42,198	52,118	28,988	53,824	7,319
April (R)	191,347	3,472	187,875	10,858	41,570	51,554	28,620	48,923	6,350
May (R)	189,913	3,248	186,665	10,453	40,761	50,356	29,431	48,880	6,785
June (R)	192,642	3,700	188,942	11,094	41,936	49,041	29,672	50,425	6,774
July (R)	189,978	2,883	187,095	10,539	42,337	49,247	30,112	47,833	7,027
August (R)	192,129	2,096	190,034	10,653	40,057	50,261	29,616	51,808	7,637
September (R)	187,849	1,973	185,877	10,729	38,469	49,267	28,794	51,472	7,145
October (R)	187,225	2,118	185,108	10,288	36,498	49,899	29,141	51,774	7,507
November (R)	183,209	2,006	181,203	10,400	36,137	49,190	29,100	48,724	7,653
December (R)	183,501	1,886	181,615	10,581	36,643	49,128	30,076	47,985	7,202
2016									
Jan. -	180,609	1,824	178,784	10,742	34,567	47,947	30,584	47,876	7,068
January	180,609	1,824	178,784	10,742	34,567	47,947	30,584	47,876	7,068
February									
March									
April									
May									
June									
July									
August									
September									
October									
November									
December									

(1) Detailed data are presented on a Census basis. The information needed to convert to a BOP basis is not available.

(2) Includes petroleum and petroleum products.

NOTE: For information on data sources, nonsampling errors, definitions, and details concerning what is included in Net Adjustments, see the informa ion section on page A-1 of this release or at www.census.gov/ft900 or www bea gov/newsreleases/interna ional/trade/tradnewsrelease htm.

Part A: Seasonally Adjusted (by Commodity/Service)

Exhibit 7. U.S. Exports of Goods by End-Use Category and Commodity

In millions of dollars. Details may not equal totals due to seasonal adjustment and rounding. The commodities in this exhibit are ranked on the monthly change within each major commodity grouping. (-) Represents zero or less than one-half of measurement shown. (R) - Revised.

Item (1)	January 2016	December 2015 (R)	Monthly Change	Year-to-Date 2016	Year-to-Date 2015 (R)	Year-to-Date Change
Total, Balance of Payments Basis	**116,890**	**120,900**	**-4,010**	**116,890**	**129,266**	**-12,375**
Net Adjustments	504	637	-133	504	805	-301
Total, Census Basis	**116,387**	**120,263**	**-3,877**	**116,387**	**128,461**	**-12,075**
Foods, feeds, and beverages	**9,429**	**9,901**	**-472**	**9,429**	**11,010**	**-1,581**
Soybeans	1,313	1,650	-337	1,313	1,987	-674
Wheat	411	504	-93	411	463	-51
Oilseeds, food oils	216	294	-78	216	283	-68
Fruits, frozen juices	626	661	-35	626	728	-102
Dairy products and eggs	294	320	-26	294	339	-44
Meat, poultry, etc.	1,284	1,309	-25	1,284	1,520	-236
Bakery products	510	531	-21	510	520	-10
Animal feeds, n.e.c.	555	573	-17	555	728	-173
Wine, beer, and related products	167	176	-9	167	161	6
Other foods	1,075	1,083	-8	1,075	1,086	-11
Nonagricultural foods, etc.	126	131	-5	126	131	-6
Rice	148	146	2	148	230	-83
Alcoholic beverages, excluding wine	166	164	2	166	168	-2
Fish and shellfish	460	457	2	460	450	10
Sorghum, barley, oats	184	175	9	184	207	-22
Corn	572	543	29	572	779	-207
Vegetables	617	555	62	617	571	46
Nuts	704	629	74	704	660	44
Industrial supplies and materials	**31,498**	**32,429**	**-932**	**31,498**	**37,573**	**-6,075**
Fuel oil	1,886	2,623	-737	1,886	3,222	-1,336
Nonmonetary gold	1,288	1,748	-460	1,288	1,921	-633
Chemicals-fertilizers	593	774	-180	593	740	-147
Gas-natural	278	365	-87	278	504	-226
Crude oil	407	487	-80	407	725	-318
Steelmaking materials	353	420	-67	353	688	-335
Chemicals-inorganic	672	714	-42	672	721	-50
Nuclear fuel materials	74	115	-41	74	128	-55
Plastic materials	2,722	2,762	-40	2,722	2,931	-209
Cotton, raw	182	212	-30	182	272	-90
Other industrial supplies	2,154	2,181	-27	2,154	2,196	-41
Newsprint	1,028	1,053	-26	1,028	1,063	-35
Aluminum and alumina	603	629	-26	603	668	-64
Industrial rubber products	366	386	-20	366	421	-55
Agric. industry-unmanufactured	311	326	-16	311	293	18
Manmade cloth	567	581	-14	567	613	-47
Nonferrous metals, other	546	560	-14	546	660	-114
Nontextile floor tiles	46	57	-11	46	48	-3
Chemicals-other	2,412	2,423	-10	2,412	2,558	-146
Metallurgical grade coal	235	244	-9	235	483	-248
Agriculture-manufactured, other	223	231	-8	223	235	-12
Finished metal shapes	1,551	1,556	-5	1,551	1,643	-92
Tapes, audio and visual	13	17	-4	13	17	-4
Wood supplies, manufactured	99	100	-1	99	113	-14
Nonmetallic minerals	79	80	-1	79	64	15
Cotton fiber cloth	186	186	1	186	209	-22
Electric energy	13	12	1	13	22	-9
Finished textile supplies	255	253	2	255	265	-10
Iron and steel products, other	523	521	2	523	656	-132
Hair, waste materials	58	54	4	58	54	3
Shingles, molding, wallboard	375	371	5	375	438	-63
Leather and furs	99	94	5	99	103	-4
Synthetic rubber-primary	278	269	9	278	300	-22
Mineral supplies-manufactured	481	470	11	481	503	-22
Coal and fuels, other	343	329	14	343	436	-93
Hides and skins	183	165	18	183	192	-9
Agric. farming-unmanufactured	256	236	19	256	271	-15
Natural gas liquids	644	625	19	644	648	-3
Glass-plate, sheet, etc.	145	125	21	145	148	-2
Tobacco, unmanufactured	92	71	22	92	83	10
Logs and lumber	487	455	32	487	469	19
Iron and steel mill products	732	692	40	732	936	-203
Pulpwood and woodpulp	746	704	42	746	761	-15
Precious metals, other	461	410	51	461	647	-186
Copper	526	422	104	526	722	-196
Chemicals-organic	2,314	2,017	297	2,314	2,472	-158
Petroleum products, other	3,611	3,306	305	3,611	4,315	-704

Part A: Seasonally Adjusted (by Commodity/Service)

Exhibit 7. U.S. Exports of Goods by End-Use Category and Commodity

In millions of dollars. Details may not equal totals due to seasonal adjustment and rounding. The commodities in this exhibit are ranked on the monthly change within each major commodity grouping. (-) Represents zero or less than one-half of measurement shown. (R) - Revised.

Item (1)	January 2016	December 2015 (R)	Monthly Change	Year-to-Date 2016	Year-to-Date 2015 (R)	Year-to-Date Change
Capital goods, except automotive	**42,801**	**44,015**	**-1,214**	**42,801**	**45,838**	**-3,037**
Drilling & oilfield equipment	475	906	-432	475	829	-355
Civilian aircraft	4,258	4,641	-383	4,258	5,506	-1,247
Telecommunications equipment	3,065	3,433	-368	3,065	3,351	-286
Industrial engines	2,187	2,461	-274	2,187	2,410	-224
Semiconductors	3,522	3,665	-144	3,522	3,772	-251
Agricultural machinery, equipment	549	635	-85	549	567	-18
Computers	1,214	1,269	-55	1,214	1,376	-162
Metalworking machine tools	547	592	-45	547	642	-95
Marine engines, parts	109	142	-33	109	127	-18
Materials handling equipment	939	969	-30	939	1,233	-294
Specialized mining	58	86	-29	58	114	-56
Nonfarm tractors and parts	181	203	-22	181	226	-45
Laboratory testing instruments	916	936	-20	916	978	-62
Excavating machinery	751	764	-13	751	1,034	-283
Industrial machines, other	4,164	4,170	-6	4,164	4,550	-386
Vessels, excluding scrap	2	3	-1	2	4	-2
Spacecraft, excluding military	1	1	(-)	1	10	-9
Pulp and paper machinery	193	191	2	193	193	(-)
Commercial vessels, other	29	26	3	29	33	-4
Textile, sewing machines	82	75	7	82	93	-11
Measuring, testing, control instruments	1,937	1,921	17	1,937	2,129	-192
Engines-civilian aircraft	3,187	3,168	19	3,187	2,738	449
Food, tobacco machinery	312	291	21	312	338	-26
Business machines and equipment	229	202	27	229	232	-3
Parts-civilian aircraft	1,909	1,882	27	1,909	1,859	51
Railway transportation equipment	320	266	54	320	266	54
Medicinal equipment	2,909	2,849	61	2,909	2,867	43
Wood, glass, plastic	353	289	64	353	343	10
Photo, service industry machinery	926	844	82	926	860	66
Computer accessories	2,616	2,525	91	2,616	2,440	177
Generators, accessories	1,197	1,073	124	1,197	1,202	-6
Electric apparatus	3,665	3,537	128	3,665	3,513	152
Automotive vehicles, parts, and engines	**12,315**	**12,296**	**19**	**12,315**	**12,783**	**-468**
Other parts and accessories of vehicles	5,111	5,062	49	5,111	4,924	188
Bodies and chassis for passenger cars	53	23	30	53	11	42
Engines and engine parts	1,416	1,405	11	1,416	1,496	-80
Passenger cars, new and used	3,952	3,942	10	3,952	4,573	-621
Automotive tires and tubes	287	295	-7	287	303	-16
Trucks, buses and special purpose vehicles	1,495	1,569	-74	1,495	1,476	19
Consumer goods	**15,979**	**16,818**	**-839**	**15,979**	**16,760**	**-781**
Artwork, antiques, stamps, etc.	678	1,328	-650	678	698	-20
Gem diamonds	1,544	1,670	-126	1,544	1,719	-175
Jewelry, etc.	959	1,021	-62	959	1,020	-61
Apparel, household goods - textile	545	599	-54	545	592	-46
Pleasure boats and motors	164	209	-46	164	188	-24
Tobacco, manufactured	80	115	-35	80	50	30
Books, printed matter	368	392	-24	368	394	-26
Furniture, household goods, etc.	393	417	-23	393	436	-43
Cell phones and other household goods, n.e.c.	1,926	1,940	-14	1,926	2,118	-192
Toiletries and cosmetics	1,002	1,014	-13	1,002	960	41
Stereo equipment, etc.	157	167	-10	157	165	-8
Musical instruments	142	148	-6	142	157	-15
Sports apparel and gear	59	65	-6	59	65	-5
Recorded media	176	176	(-)	176	213	-37
Nursery stock, etc.	35	35	(-)	35	30	5
Apparel,household goods-nontextile	261	260	2	261	252	9
Glassware, chinaware	50	48	2	50	49	2
Other consumer nondurables	606	604	2	606	639	-32
Cookware, cutlery, tools	103	101	3	103	94	9
Rugs	88	84	4	88	94	-6
Household appliances	600	583	17	600	622	-22
Toys, games, and sporting goods	809	782	27	809	855	-46
Numismatic coins	103	74	29	103	124	-21
Pharmaceutical preparations	4,698	4,642	56	4,698	4,746	-48
Televisions and video equipment	433	344	89	433	483	-50
Other goods	**4,365**	**4,804**	**-440**	**4,365**	**4,497**	**-132**

(1) Detailed data are presented on a Census basis. The information needed to convert to a BOP basis is not available.

NOTE: For information on data sources, nonsampling errors, definitions, and details concerning what is included in Net Adjustments, see the information section on page A-1 of this release or at www.census.gov/ft900 or www.bea.gov/newsreleases/international/trade/tradnewsrelease.htm.

Part A: Seasonally Adjusted (by Commodity/Service)

Exhibit 8. U.S. Imports of Goods by End-Use Category and Commodity

In millions of dollars. Details may not equal totals due to seasonal adjustment and rounding. The commodities in this exhibit are ranked on the monthly change within each major commodity grouping. (-) Represents zero or less than one-half of measurement shown. (R) - Revised.

Item (1)	January 2016	December 2015 (R)	Monthly Change	Year-to-Date 2016	Year-to-Date 2015 (R)	Year-to-Date Change
Total, Balance of Payments Basis	**180,609**	**183,501**	**-2,892**	**180,609**	**192,244**	**-11,635**
Net Adjustments	1,824	1,886	-62	1,824	2,685	-860
Total, Census Basis	**178,784**	**181,615**	**-2,830**	**178,784**	**189,559**	**-10,775**
Foods, feeds, and beverages	**10,742**	**10,581**	**161**	**10,742**	**10,673**	**69**
Alcoholic beverages, excluding wine	702	573	129	702	672	30
Meat products	970	848	122	970	1,120	-150
Wine, beer, and related products	925	875	50	925	803	121
Dairy products and eggs	199	155	44	199	165	34
Cane and beet sugar	160	118	42	160	146	14
Bakery products	872	832	39	872	783	88
Cocoa beans	145	122	23	145	128	16
Vegetables	1,046	1,030	16	1,046	883	163
Fish and shellfish	1,561	1,550	10	1,561	1,707	-147
Food oils, oilseeds	521	517	5	521	520	1
Nonagricultural foods, etc.	80	79	1	80	97	-17
Nuts	240	253	-12	240	207	33
Tea, spices, etc.	183	206	-23	183	174	9
Fruits, frozen juices	1,311	1,338	-27	1,311	1,261	50
Green coffee	329	366	-37	329	348	-19
Feedstuff and foodgrains	498	537	-39	498	551	-53
Other foods	1,000	1,182	-182	1,000	1,106	-106
Industrial supplies and materials	**34,567**	**36,643**	**-2,076**	**34,567**	**46,697**	**-12,130**
Crude oil	7,597	9,445	-1,848	7,597	13,366	-5,769
Iron and steel mill products	1,220	1,452	-233	1,220	2,305	-1,086
Nonmonetary gold	739	963	-224	739	935	-196
Other precious metals	552	709	-158	552	885	-333
Coal and related fuels	98	217	-119	98	170	-72
Chemicals-inorganic	502	551	-50	502	623	-121
Steelmaking materials	315	363	-49	315	801	-486
Chemicals-fertilizers	967	1,014	-46	967	1,170	-203
Chemicals-organic	1,779	1,821	-43	1,779	2,222	-443
Shingles, wallboard	837	871	-34	837	824	13
Synthetic cloth	482	511	-29	482	554	-71
Tobacco, waxes, etc.	641	667	-26	641	785	-144
Pulpwood and woodpulp	243	268	-25	243	278	-35
Liquefied petroleum gases	140	162	-21	140	305	-165
Sulfur, nonmetallic minerals	90	110	-19	90	129	-38
Iron and steel, advanced	784	799	-14	784	882	-98
Farming materials, livestock	176	189	-13	176	151	26
Glass-plate, sheet, etc.	139	150	-11	139	132	7
Zinc	93	102	-10	93	133	-40
Hides and skins	10	18	-8	10	13	-3
Petroleum products, other	2,116	2,121	-5	2,116	3,051	-935
Cotton cloth, fabrics	87	90	-3	87	89	-2
Finished textile supplies	396	398	-2	396	398	-2
Newsprint	82	83	-1	82	97	-15
Nontextile floor tiles	328	329	-1	328	272	57
Materials, excluding chemicals	117	117	1	117	136	-18
Cotton, natural fibers	8	7	1	8	5	3
Synthetic rubber--primary	190	189	1	190	222	-32
Hair, waste materials	84	82	3	84	89	-4
Leather and furs	64	62	3	64	70	-6
Blank tapes, audio & visual	41	38	4	41	51	-10
Natural rubber	108	104	4	108	136	-29
Copper	302	297	4	302	507	-205
Wool, silk, etc.	68	63	5	68	61	7
Tin	46	41	5	46	71	-25
Chemicals-other, n.e.c.	1,002	997	5	1,002	1,035	-34
Paper and paper products	619	613	6	619	629	-10
Stone, sand, cement, etc.	480	472	8	480	465	15
Nickel	126	110	16	126	235	-109
Plywood and veneers	250	227	23	250	236	13
Industrial supplies, o her	2,651	2,612	39	2,651	2,643	9
Lumber	519	478	40	519	507	12
Iron and steel products, n.e.c.	744	701	43	744	978	-234
Gas-natural	484	438	46	484	793	-309
Nonferrous metals, other	311	264	47	311	327	-16
Plastic materials	1,340	1,280	60	1,340	1,469	-129
Electric energy	194	125	69	194	167	27
Bauxite and aluminum	997	901	96	997	1,125	-128
Finished metal shapes	1,675	1,553	122	1,675	1,500	175
Fuel oil	1,333	1,206	127	1,333	2,502	-1,169
Nuclear fuel materials	401	261	140	401	168	233

Part A: Seasonally Adjusted (by Commodity/Service)

Exhibit 8. U.S. Imports of Goods by End-Use Category and Commodity

In millions of dollars. Details may not equal totals due to seasonal adjustment and rounding. The commodities in this exhibit are ranked on the monthly change within each major commodity grouping. (-) Represents zero or less than one-half of measurement shown. (R) - Revised.

Item (1)	January 2016	December 2015 (R)	Monthly Change	Year-to-Date 2016	Year-to-Date 2015 (R)	Year-to-Date Change
Capital goods, except automotive	**47,947**	**49,128**	**-1,181**	**47,947**	**50,417**	**-2,469**
Civilian aircraft	820	1,732	-911	820	1,432	-612
Telecommunications equipment	5,477	5,881	-404	5,477	5,112	365
Computers	4,664	4,992	-328	4,664	4,996	-332
Agricultural machinery, equipment	777	847	-70	777	830	-53
Industrial engines	1,910	1,975	-65	1,910	2,068	-158
Engines-civilian aircraft	1,658	1,715	-57	1,658	1,629	29
Measuring, testing, control instruments	1,645	1,701	-56	1,645	1,725	-80
Nonfarm tractors and parts	116	148	-32	116	158	-43
Laboratory testing instruments	450	480	-30	450	518	-68
Spacecraft, excluding military	2	14	-12	2	3	-1
Food, tobacco machinery	313	325	-12	313	306	7
Wood, glass, plastic	659	669	-10	659	632	26
Medicinal equipment	3,028	3,035	-7	3,028	2,856	171
Marine engines, parts	113	118	-6	113	89	24
Railway transportation equipment	113	116	-4	113	142	-29
Specialized mining	54	55	-2	54	77	-23
Industrial machines, other	4,202	4,202	-1	4,202	4,724	-523
Vessels, except scrap	(-)	(-)	(-)	(-)	(-)	(-)
Commercial vessels, other	8	7	1	8	7	1
Metalworking machine tools	877	856	21	877	958	-81
Pulp and paper machinery	431	405	26	431	346	85
Textile, sewing machines	192	166	26	192	206	-14
Parts-civilian aircraft	1,425	1,395	30	1,425	1,449	-24
Business machines and equipment	425	394	31	425	382	43
Semiconductors	4,156	4,123	32	4,156	3,538	618
Electric apparatus	3,982	3,939	43	3,982	4,211	-230
Drilling & oilfield equipment	306	257	49	306	1,221	-914
Materials handling equipment	1,322	1,271	51	1,322	1,403	-81
Excava ing machinery	775	714	62	775	1,103	-328
Photo, service industry machinery	1,632	1,497	135	1,632	1,491	140
Computer accessories	4,415	4,258	157	4,415	4,873	-459
Generators, accessories	2,002	1,841	161	2,002	1,929	73
Automotive vehicles, parts, and engines	**30,584**	**30,076**	**508**	**30,584**	**28,110**	**2,475**
Trucks, buses, and special purpose vehicles	3,038	2,682	356	3,038	2,894	144
Other parts and accessories of vehicles	9,056	8,821	236	9,056	8,305	752
Passenger cars, new and used	15,116	15,067	49	15,116	13,535	1,582
Bodies and chassis for trucks and buses	64	60	4	64	65	(-)
Bodies and chassis for passenger cars	2	2	(-)	2	2	1
Automotive tires and tubes	1,020	1,029	-9	1,020	1,026	-6
Engines and engine parts	2,287	2,415	-128	2,287	2,284	3
Consumer goods	**47,876**	**47,985**	**-108**	**47,876**	**47,177**	**700**
Pharmaceutical preparations	8,178	8,900	-722	8,178	7,883	295
Furniture, household goods, etc.	2,716	2,907	-191	2,716	2,517	198
Apparel, household goods - cotton	3,765	3,868	-103	3,765	3,714	51
Pleasure boats and motors	237	330	-93	237	470	-233
Camping apparel and gear	942	1,026	-84	942	858	84
Numismatic coins	158	227	-69	158	108	49
Motorcycles and parts	258	316	-59	258	264	-6
Apparel, textiles, nonwool or cotton	4,026	4,078	-52	4,026	3,726	300
Footwear	1,660	1,696	-37	1,660	1,509	151
Books, printed matter	324	340	-16	324	313	11
Televisions and video equipment	2,112	2,124	-12	2,112	2,147	-35
Jewelry	1,196	1,199	-3	1,196	1,142	54
Apparel,household goods-nontextile	749	750	(-)	749	746	3
Apparel, household goods - wool	269	267	2	269	266	3
Recorded media	78	72	6	78	68	10
Musical instruments	145	136	10	145	132	13
Stereo equipment, etc	506	495	11	506	477	29
Nursery stock, etc.	153	139	13	153	136	17
Artwork, antiques, stamps, etc.	900	879	20	900	1,126	-227
Glassware, chinaware	227	206	21	227	187	40
Rugs	219	196	23	219	208	11
Other consumer nondurables	1,249	1,223	25	1,249	1,191	57
Household appliances	2,285	2,257	28	2,285	2,169	117
Cookware, cutlery, tools	782	746	36	782	683	98
Toys, games, and sporting goods	2,896	2,858	38	2,896	2,751	145
Toiletries and cosmetics	933	853	79	933	855	78
Gem stones, other	384	293	91	384	343	41
Gem diamonds	1,971	1,832	139	1,971	1,923	48
Photo equipment	445	281	164	445	344	100
Cell phones and other household goods, n.e.c.	8,114	7,489	626	8,114	8,920	-805
Other goods	**7,068**	**7,202**	**-134**	**7,068**	**6,487**	**581**

(1) Detailed data are presented on a Census basis. The information needed to convert to a BOP basis is not available.

NOTE: For information on data sources, nonsampling errors, definitions, and details concerning what is included in Net Adjustments, see the information section on page A-1 of this release or at www.census.gov/ft900 or www.bea.gov/newsreleases/international/trade/tradnewsrelease.htm.

Part A: Seasonally Adjusted (by Commodity/Service)

Exhibit 9. U.S. Trade in Petroleum and Non-Petroleum Products by End-Use

In millions of dollars. Details may not equal totals due to seasonal adjustment and rounding. (R) - Revised.

Period	Balance				Exports				Imports			
	Total	Net Adjust-ments	Petroleum (1)	Non-petroleum	Total	Net Adjust-ments	Petroleum (1)	Non-petroleum	Total	Net Adjust-ments	Petroleum (1)	Non-petroleum
2015												
Jan. - Dec. (R)	-759,307	-23,288	-82,505	-653,514	1,513,453	8,539	99,476	1,405,438	2,272,760	31,828	181,980	2,058,952
Jan. - (R)	-62,978	-1,880	-10,315	-50,783	129,266	805	8,909	119,552	192,244	2,685	19,225	170,335
January (R)	-62,978	-1,880	-10,315	-50,783	129,266	805	8,909	119,552	192,244	2,685	19,225	170,335
February (R)	-58,069	-2,101	-8,090	-47,878	126,303	714	8,284	117,305	184,372	2,815	16,374	165,184
March (R)	-71,192	-1,903	-7,548	-61,742	127,157	1,043	7,654	118,460	198,349	2,946	15,202	180,202
April (R)	-62,027	-2,592	-6,851	-52,583	129,320	880	8,541	119,899	191,347	3,472	15,392	172,482
May (R)	-62,105	-2,496	-5,780	-53,828	127,808	752	9,544	117,512	189,913	3,248	15,325	171,340
June (R)	-65,143	-2,793	-7,333	-55,017	127,499	907	9,414	117,178	192,642	3,700	16,748	172,195
July (R)	-61,475	-2,175	-8,134	-51,166	128,503	708	8,950	118,845	189,978	2,883	17,084	170,011
August (R)	-67,884	-1,610	-6,982	-59,291	124,246	485	8,118	115,642	192,129	2,096	15,101	174,933
September (R)	-61,153	-1,688	-5,596	-53,868	126,697	285	8,256	118,156	187,849	1,973	13,852	172,025
October (R)	-63,189	-1,342	-4,519	-57,328	124,037	775	7,515	115,746	187,225	2,118	12,034	173,074
November (R)	-61,492	-1,459	-5,464	-54,570	121,717	547	7,248	113,921	183,209	2,006	12,712	168,491
December (R)	-62,600	-1,249	-5,892	-55,460	120,900	637	7,041	113,222	183,501	1,886	12,933	168,681
2016												
Jan. -	-63,718	-1,320	-4,638	-57,760	116,890	504	6,548	109,838	180,609	1,824	11,186	167,598
January	-63,718	-1,320	-4,638	-57,760	116,890	504	6,548	109,838	180,609	1,824	11,186	167,598
February												
March												
April												
May												
June												
July												
August												
September												
October												
November												
December												

(1) The petroleum products aggregated in the end-use commodity classification system include virtually the same energy-related petroleum products as those aggregated in the Standard International Trade Classification (SITC). The end-use petroleum products, however, include some products such as ethane, butane, benzene, and toluene, which are included in "Manufactured Goods" in the SITC.

NOTE: For information on data sources, nonsampling errors, definitions, and details concerning what is included in Net Adjustments, see the information section on page A-1 of this release or at www.census.gov/ft900 or www.bea.gov/newsreleases/international/trade/tradnewsrelease.htm.

Part A: Seasonally Adjusted (by Commodity/Service)

Exhibit 10. Real U.S. Trade in Goods by Principal End-Use Category Chained (2009) Dollars

In millions of dollars. Details may not equal totals due to seasonal adjustment and rounding. The values in this exhibit are subject to periodic change, reflecting revisions to the source information for the monthly deflators. (-) Represents zero or less than one-half of measurement shown. (R) - Revised.

Period	Total Census Basis (1)	End-Use Commodity Category						
		Foods, Feeds, & Beverages	Industrial Supplies (2)	Capital Goods	Automotive Vehicles etc.	Consumer Goods	Other Goods	Residual (3)
	Exports							
2015								
Jan. - Dec. (R)	1,437,331	110,735	399,508	534,444	144,889	196,814	57,429	-6,489
Jan. - (R)	120,556	8,863	34,165	45,323	12,203	16,501	4,138	-636
January (R)	120,556	8,863	34,165	45,323	12,203	16,501	4,138	-636
February (R)	118,000	8,915	32,773	43,820	11,227	17,606	4,298	-638
March (R)	118,719	9,240	32,738	44,729	11,799	15,999	4,773	-558
April (R)	121,755	9,224	33,800	46,864	11,955	15,972	4,563	-622
May (R)	119,562	9,465	33,731	44,408	12,059	15,869	4,513	-483
June (R)	119,604	9,300	33,250	43,803	12,091	16,606	5,071	-517
July (R)	121,155	9,185	34,105	44,045	12,689	16,228	5,385	-482
August (R)	119,119	9,247	33,389	44,130	12,201	15,729	4,910	-487
September (R)	122,578	9,763	34,008	45,052	12,358	17,020	4,880	-505
October (R)	119,521	9,182	32,449	44,131	12,221	16,534	5,511	-507
November (R)	118,171	9,314	32,237	44,204	12,311	15,859	4,741	-494
December (R)	118,590	9,037	32,861	43,934	11,777	16,892	4,646	-557
2016								
Jan. -	116,023	8,755	32,801	42,827	11,808	16,128	4,266	-563
January	116,023	8,755	32,801	42,827	11,808	16,128	4,266	-563
February								
March								
April								
May								
June								
July								
August								
September								
October								
November								
December								
	Imports							
2015								
Jan. - Dec. (R)	2,141,062	100,763	466,548	621,788	339,525	579,666	80,573	-47,801
Jan. - (R)	174,890	8,350	39,457	51,704	27,225	45,949	6,074	-3,868
January (R)	174,890	8,350	39,457	51,704	27,225	45,949	6,074	-3,868
February (R)	170,266	8,042	38,553	50,047	25,855	45,092	6,415	-3,739
March (R)	185,211	8,550	39,806	53,633	28,202	52,303	6,905	-4,188
April (R)	178,818	8,537	39,586	53,195	27,903	47,623	6,019	-4,044
May (R)	177,167	8,198	38,309	52,027	28,675	47,576	6,427	-4,045
June (R)	178,627	8,729	38,411	50,910	28,951	49,081	6,431	-3,887
July (R)	177,214	8,286	38,941	51,274	29,332	46,631	6,685	-3,935
August (R)	182,032	8,359	38,753	52,298	28,903	50,524	7,282	-4,088
September (R)	180,132	8,485	39,244	51,347	28,106	50,117	6,824	-3,992
October (R)	180,632	8,308	38,138	52,110	28,475	50,417	7,196	-4,014
November (R)	177,398	8,365	38,112	51,598	28,450	47,485	7,360	-3,973
December (R)	178,676	8,552	39,238	51,646	29,448	46,867	6,953	-4,029
2016								
Jan. -	177,996	8,687	39,230	50,388	30,001	46,771	6,843	-3,923
January	177,996	8,687	39,230	50,388	30,001	46,771	6,843	-3,923
February								
March								
April								
May								
June								
July								
August								
September								
October								
November								
December								

(1) Detailed data are presented on a Census basis. The information needed to convert to a BOP basis is not available.
(2) Includes petroleum and petroleum products.
(3) The "residual" represents the difference between total exports or imports of goods on a Census basis and the sum of the components. For additional information, see www.census.gov/foreign-trade/aip/priceadj.html.

NOTE: For information on data sources, nonsampling errors, and definitions, see the information section on page A-1 of this release or at www.census gov/ft900 or www.bea.gov/newsreleases/international/trade/tradnewsrelease htm.

Part A: Seasonally Adjusted (by Commodity/Service)

Exhibit 11. Real U.S. Trade in Petroleum and Non-Petroleum Products by End-Use Chained (2009) Dollars

In millions of dollars. Details may not equal totals due to seasonal adjustment and rounding. The values in this exhibit are subject to periodic change, reflecting revisions to the source information for the monthly deflators. (-) Represents zero or less than one-half of measurement shown. (R) - Revised.

Period	Balance				Exports				Imports			
	Total Census Basis (1)	Petroleum	Non-petroleum	Residual (2)	Total Census Basis (1)	Petroleum	Non-petroleum	Residual (2)	Total Census Basis (1)	Petroleum	Non-petroleum	Residual (2)
2014												
Jan. - Dec.	-601,598	-114,897	-552,284	65,583	1,444,790	90,625	1,343,992	10,173	2,046,388	205,522	1,896,276	-55,410
Jan. -	-49,068	-10,781	-42,794	4,507	116,986	6,977	109,346	663	166,054	17,758	152,140	-3,843
January	-49,068	-10,781	-42,794	4,507	116,986	6,977	109,346	663	166,054	17,758	152,140	-3,843
February	-49,190	-11,232	-42,143	4,184	115,780	6,495	108,867	418	164,970	17,727	151,010	-3,766
March	-51,198	-11,251	-44,442	4,495	118,332	6,642	111,260	430	169,530	17,893	155,702	-4,065
April	-52,318	-10,389	-47,029	5,100	118,860	7,201	110,943	716	171,178	17,591	157,972	-4,384
May	-51,287	-9,137	-47,895	5,744	120,137	7,927	111,171	1,039	171,424	17,064	159,066	-4,706
June	-49,756	-8,364	-47,440	6,048	119,801	7,859	110,927	1,014	169,557	16,223	158,368	-5,034
July	-48,346	-8,228	-46,179	6,061	121,428	8,255	112,008	1,165	169,775	16,483	158,187	-4,896
August	-48,820	-8,140	-46,859	6,180	122,288	8,494	112,536	1,259	171,108	16,635	159,395	-4,921
September	-49,987	-8,676	-47,294	5,983	121,196	7,758	112,488	950	171,182	16,434	159,782	-5,033
October	-49,906	-9,722	-45,831	5,647	123,640	7,155	115,835	650	173,547	16,877	161,666	-4,996
November	-48,592	-8,326	-46,324	6,059	123,093	7,951	114,203	940	171,685	16,277	160,527	-5,119
December	-53,130	-10,651	-48,054	5,575	123,247	7,911	114,408	929	176,377	18,562	162,462	-4,646
2015												
Jan. - Dec. (R)	-703,731	-109,225	-663,776	69,270	1,437,331	96,446	1,329,447	11,438	2,141,062	205,671	1,993,223	-57,832
Jan. - (R)	-54,334	-8,697	-51,401	5,764	120,556	8,602	110,989	965	174,890	17,299	162,389	-4,799
January (R)	-54,334	-8,697	-51,401	5,764	120,556	8,602	110,989	965	174,890	17,299	162,389	-4,799
February (R)	-52,266	-9,511	-48,382	5,627	118,000	7,596	109,451	953	170,266	17,107	157,832	-4,674
March (R)	-66,492	-10,274	-62,060	5,842	118,719	6,836	110,950	933	185,211	17,110	173,010	-4,910
April (R)	-57,063	-9,207	-53,691	5,835	121,755	8,118	112,659	978	178,818	17,325	166,350	-4,857
May (R)	-57,605	-8,372	-54,949	5,716	119,562	8,269	110,322	971	177,167	16,642	165,271	-4,745
June (R)	-59,023	-8,769	-56,014	5,760	119,604	8,173	110,469	963	178,627	16,941	166,483	-4,798
July (R)	-56,059	-9,207	-52,591	5,739	121,155	8,052	112,143	960	177,214	17,259	164,734	-4,779
August (R)	-62,913	-8,906	-59,793	5,786	119,119	8,073	110,102	944	182,032	16,979	169,895	-4,842
September (R)	-57,555	-9,003	-54,461	5,909	122,578	8,728	112,907	942	180,132	17,731	167,369	-4,967
October (R)	-61,111	-8,335	-58,328	5,552	119,521	7,869	110,675	977	180,632	16,204	169,003	-4,575
November (R)	-59,227	-9,461	-55,585	5,819	118,171	7,744	109,458	969	177,398	17,205	165,042	-4,849
December (R)	-60,085	-9,484	-56,523	5,922	118,590	8,384	109,321	885	178,676	17,868	165,844	-5,036
2016												
Jan. -	-61,973	-9,093	-58,646	5,765	116,023	8,694	106,577	752	177,996	17,787	165,222	-5,013
January	-61,973	-9,093	-58,646	5,765	116,023	8,694	106,577	752	177,996	17,787	165,222	-5,013
February												
March												
April												
May												
June												
July												
August												
September												
October												
November												
December												

(1) Detailed data are presented on a Census basis. The information needed to convert to a BOP basis is not available.

(2) The "residual" represents the difference between total exports or imports of goods on a Census basis and the sum of the components. For additional information, see www.census.gov/foreign-trade/aip/priceadj.html.

NOTE: For information on data sources, nonsampling errors, and definitions, see the information section on page A-1 of this release or at www.census.gov/ft900 or www.bea.gov/newsreleases/international/trade/tradnewsrelease.htm.

Part B: NOT Seasonally Adjusted

Exhibit 12. U.S. Trade in Goods

In millions of dollars. Details may not equal totals due to rounding. (R) - Revised.

Period	Balance		Exports			Imports		
	Total Balance of Payments Basis	Total Census Basis	Total Balance of Payments Basis	Net Adjustments	Total Census Basis	Total Balance of Payments Basis	Net Adjustments	Total Census Basis
2014								
Jan. - Dec.	-741,462	-727,153	1,632,639	12,107	1,620,532	2,374,101	26,416	2,347,685
Jan. -	-59,835	-59,098	128,035	1,518	126,517	187,870	2,255	185,615
January	-59,835	-59,098	128,035	1,518	126,517	187,870	2,255	185,615
February	-48,420	-46,649	124,128	537	123,591	172,548	2,308	170,240
March	-53,168	-51,890	143,375	1,192	142,184	196,544	2,469	194,074
April	-67,768	-66,708	135,028	1,154	133,875	202,796	2,214	200,582
May	-62,912	-62,060	139,420	1,298	138,122	202,332	2,150	200,182
June	-60,319	-59,319	139,557	1,199	138,358	199,876	2,199	197,677
July	-72,001	-71,124	134,503	1,305	133,198	206,504	2,182	204,322
August	-60,548	-59,174	138,244	825	137,420	198,792	2,199	196,594
September	-70,948	-69,527	134,107	746	133,360	205,055	2,168	202,887
October	-66,452	-65,214	146,351	915	145,436	212,803	2,153	210,650
November	-56,110	-55,007	135,695	969	134,726	191,805	2,072	189,733
December	-62,981	-61,384	134,196	450	133,746	197,177	2,048	195,129
2015								
Jan. - Dec. (R)	-759,307	-736,019	1,513,453	8,539	1,504,914	2,272,760	31,828	2,240,933
Jan. -	-60,636	-58,716	122,126	728	121,398	182,761	2,648	180,113
January	-60,636	-58,716	122,126	728	121,398	182,761	2,648	180,113
February	-46,011	-43,899	118,980	632	118,348	164,991	2,744	162,246
March	-65,102	-63,102	134,778	993	133,785	199,880	2,993	196,886
April	-62,944	-60,367	129,394	889	128,505	192,338	3,465	188,872
May	-59,407	-56,932	129,023	764	128,259	188,430	3,239	185,191
June	-67,668	-64,939	131,937	943	130,994	199,605	3,672	195,933
July (R)	-70,641	-68,527	125,157	766	124,391	195,798	2,880	192,918
August (R)	-68,664	-67,084	123,562	551	123,011	192,226	2,131	190,095
September (R)	-67,855	-66,166	125,603	321	125,281	193,458	2,011	191,447
October (R)	-66,490	-65,036	131,249	787	130,463	197,740	2,241	195,499
November (R)	-62,935	-61,486	121,102	532	120,570	184,037	1,981	182,056
December (R)	-60,954	-59,765	120,543	634	119,909	181,497	1,823	179,674
2016								
Jan. -	-58,734	-57,394	108,892	439	108,453	167,626	1,778	165,848
January	-58,734	-57,394	108,892	439	108,453	167,626	1,778	165,848
February								
March								
April								
May								
June								
July								
August								
September								
October								
November								
December								
December data as published last month:	-60,867	-59,918	120,796	887	119,909	181,663	1,835	179,828

NOTE: For informa ion on data sources, nonsampling errors, definitions, and details concerning what is included in Net Adjustments, see the information section on page A-1 of this release or at www.census.gov/ft900 or www.bea.gov/newsreleases/international/trade/tradnewsrelease.htm.

Part B: NOT Seasonally Adjusted

Exhibit 13. U.S. Trade in Goods by Principal End-Use Category

In millions of dollars. Details may not equal totals due to rounding. (R) - Revised.

Period	Total Balance of Payments Basis	Net Adjustments	Total Census Basis (1)	End-Use Commodity Category: Foods, Feeds, & Beverages	Industrial Supplies (2)	Capital Goods	Automotive Vehicles, etc.	Consumer Goods	Other Goods
Exports									
2015									
Jan. - Dec. (R)	1,513,453	8,539	1,504,914	127,704	428,172	538,341	151,563	197,817	61,317
Jan. -	122,126	728	121,398	11,657	36,439	42,593	10,705	15,556	4,448
January	122,126	728	121,398	11,657	36,439	42,593	10,705	15,556	4,448
February	118,980	632	118,348	10,831	34,322	40,271	11,179	17,135	4,610
March	134,778	993	133,785	11,351	38,245	48,221	13,571	17,197	5,199
April	129,394	889	128,505	10,263	37,914	46,667	12,972	15,781	4,907
May	129,023	764	128,259	9,959	38,454	45,215	13,522	16,204	4,905
June	131,937	943	130,994	9,330	37,303	46,342	13,496	19,028	5,496
July (R)	125,157	766	124,391	9,418	37,831	44,050	11,688	15,616	5,789
August (R)	123,562	551	123,011	9,538	35,668	44,452	13,115	15,012	5,225
September (R)	125,603	321	125,281	9,766	34,498	45,370	13,234	17,300	5,113
October (R)	131,249	787	130,463	12,527	34,184	46,662	13,610	17,660	5,819
November (R)	121,102	532	120,570	12,242	31,570	42,995	13,127	15,670	4,966
December (R)	120,543	634	119,909	10,822	31,744	45,502	11,345	15,657	4,839
2016									
Jan. -	108,892	439	108,453	9,619	30,111	39,455	10,255	14,697	4,316
January	108,892	439	108,453	9,619	30,111	39,455	10,255	14,697	4,316
February									
March									
April									
May									
June									
July									
August									
September									
October									
November									
December									
Imports									
2015									
Jan. - Dec. (R)	2,272,760	31,828	2,240,933	127,689	485,908	599,156	348,283	595,175	84,721
Jan. -	182,761	2,648	180,113	10,728	46,020	47,080	25,012	44,935	6,339
January	182,761	2,648	180,113	10,728	46,020	47,080	25,012	44,935	6,339
February	164,991	2,744	162,246	9,513	38,624	42,655	24,840	40,379	6,235
March	199,880	2,993	196,886	11,679	43,550	53,674	30,812	49,672	7,499
April	192,338	3,465	188,872	11,157	43,344	51,382	29,412	46,976	6,601
May	188,430	3,239	185,191	10,718	41,970	49,833	28,908	47,403	6,360
June	199,605	3,672	195,933	11,456	43,799	52,216	30,571	50,774	7,117
July (R)	195,798	2,880	192,918	10,484	44,628	51,100	29,117	50,404	7,186
August (R)	192,226	2,131	190,095	10,235	40,444	49,791	30,095	52,296	7,233
September (R)	193,458	2,011	191,447	10,187	38,609	49,769	28,480	56,811	7,591
October (R)	197,740	2,241	195,499	10,454	36,303	51,667	31,118	58,128	7,828
November (R)	184,037	1,981	182,056	10,246	33,655	49,738	30,161	50,871	7,386
December (R)	181,497	1,823	179,674	10,831	34,962	50,251	29,758	46,526	7,346
2016									
Jan. -	167,626	1,778	165,848	10,612	33,378	43,848	26,743	44,607	6,659
January	167,626	1,778	165,848	10,612	33,378	43,848	26,743	44,607	6,659
February									
March									
April									
May									
June									
July									
August									
September									
October									
November									
December									

(1) Detailed data are presented on a Census basis. The information needed to convert to a BOP basis is not available.

(2) Includes petroleum and petroleum products.

NOTE: For information on data sources, nonsampling errors, definitions, and details concerning what is included in Net Adjustments, see the informa ion section on page A-1 of this release or at www.census.gov/ft900 or www bea gov/newsreleases/interna ional/trade/tradnewsrelease htm.

Part B: NOT Seasonally Adjusted

Exhibit 14. U.S. Trade in Goods by Selected Countries and Areas

In millions of dollars. Details may not equal totals due to rounding. (-) Represents zero or less than one-half of measurement shown.
(R) - Revised. (X) - Not applicable.

Item (1)	Balance			Exports			Imports		
	January 2016		December 2015	January 2016		December 2015	January 2016		December 2015
Total Balance of Payments Basis	**-58,734**	**(R)**	**-60,954**	**108,892**	**(R)**	**120,543**	**167,626**	**(R)**	**181,497**
Net Adjustments	-1,339	(R)	-1,189	439	(R)	634	1,778	(R)	1,823
Total Census Basis	**-57,394**	**(R)**	**-59,765**	**108,453**	**(R)**	**119,909**	**165,848**	**(R)**	**179,674**
North America	-6,700		-6,751	37,865		39,998	44,565		46,750
Canada	-2,365		-2,171	19,799		21,418	22,164		23,589
Mexico	-4,335		-4,580	18,066		18,581	22,401		23,161
Europe	-10,106		-14,924	23,553		25,826	33,659		40,750
European Union	-8,833		-13,717	20,455		21,807	29,288		35,524
Austria	351		-636	1,083		266	732		902
Belgium	1,302		917	2,581		2,473	1,279		1,555
Czech Republic	-131		-236	183		154	314		391
Finland	-180		-189	110		109	291		298
France	-1,051		-1,540	2,244		2,454	3,295		3,994
Germany	-4,542		-6,733	3,697		4,004	8,239		10,737
Hungary	-277		-392	154		167	431		559
Ireland	-2,390		-2,943	734		625	3,124		3,568
Italy	-1,993		-2,255	1,203		1,503	3,196		3,758
Netherlands	1,572		2,088	2,663		3,524	1,092		1,435
Poland	-136		-150	286		325	421		475
Spain	-84		-300	847		816	931		1,116
Sweden	-460		-588	238		320	699		908
United Kingdom	271		196	3,920		4,326	3,649		4,131
O her	-1,085		-957	512		741	1,597		1,698
Norway	-64		115	272		431	337		316
Russia	-597		-429	363		476	960		906
Switzerland	-698		-1,310	1,466		1,832	2,165		3,142
Other Europe	87		417	996		1,279	910		862
Euro Area	-7,390		-11,995	15,457		16,212	22,847		28,207
Pacific Rim Countries	-36,583		-35,608	27,013		30,600	63,596		66,208
Australia	693		1,106	1,518		1,931	825		825
China	-28,934		-27,888	8,212		10,127	37,146		38,015
Indonesia	-829		-907	731		596	1,560		1,503
Japan	-4,882		-6,555	4,702		4,766	9,583		11,321
Malaysia	-1,544		-1,983	935		956	2,479		2,940
Philippines	-110		-181	610		597	720		778
Newly Industrialized Countries (NICs)	-908		798	10,020		11,308	10,928		10,510
Hong Kong	2,188		2,916	2,673		3,398	485		482
Korea, Sou h	-2,724		-1,996	3,187		3,391	5,912		5,387
Singapore	749		1,138	2,028		2,578	1,279		1,440
Taiwan	-1,121		-1,260	2,132		1,941	3,252		3,201
Other	-70		1	285		318	356		317
South/Central America	3,098		2,809	10,597		11,697	7,499		8,888
Argentina	405		371	678		734	273		363
Brazil	363		148	2,087		2,398	1,724		2,250
Chile	440		728	1,251		1,343	811		614
Colombia	117		174	1,022		1,295	905		1,121
Other	1,772		1,388	5,559		5,927	3,786		4,539
OPEC	-364		574	5,217		5,848	5,581		5,274
Nigeria	-47		45	131		236	178		191
Saudi Arabia	-353		-108	1,159		1,746	1,511		1,854
Venezuela	-277		-618	389		366	666		984
Other (3)	312		1,255	3,538		3,500	3,226		2,246
Africa	-357		-102	1,523		1,898	1,881		2,000
Algeria	-57		18	111		159	168		141
Egypt	111		260	238		368	127		108
South Africa	-261		-247	308		417	569		664
Other	-150		-133	866		954	1,017		1,088
Other Countries	-7,792		-6,752	4,627		5,288	12,420		12,041
India	-2,191		-1,475	1,489		1,545	3,680		3,020
Thailand	-1,452		-1,418	742		931	2,194		2,349
Other	-4,149		-3,859	2,396		2,812	6,546		6,672
Unidentified Countries (2)	(-)		(-)	(-)		(-)	(X)		(X)
Timing Adjustments	(X)		153	(X)		(-)	(X)		-154

(1) Detailed data are presented on a Census basis. The information needed to convert to a BOP basis is not available.
(2) The export totals reflect shipments of certain grains, oilseeds, and satellites that are not included in the country/area totals.
(3) January statistics include Indonesia, which rejoined OPEC on January 1, 2016.

NOTES:
* This exhibit is not additive; countries may be included in more than one area. For a list of countries in each area, see the information sec ion on page A-1 of this release or at www.census.gov/ft900 or www.bea.gov/newsreleases/international/trade/tradnewsrelease.htm.
* Area data reflect the composition of the areas at the time of reporting.
* For information on data sources, nonsampling errors, definitions, and details concerning what is included in Net Adjustments, see the information section on page A-1 of this release or at www.census gov/ft900 or www.bea.gov/newsreleases/international/trade/tradnewsrelease.htm.

Part B: NOT Seasonally Adjusted

Exhibit 14a. U.S. Trade in Goods by Selected Countries and Areas

In millions of dollars. Details may not equal totals due to rounding. (-) Represents zero or less than one-half of measurement shown.
(X) - Not applicable.

Item (1)	Balance		Exports		Imports	
	January 2015	December 2014	January 2015	December 2014	January 2015	December 2014
Total Balance of Payments Basis	**-60,636**	**-62,981**	**122,126**	**134,196**	**182,761**	**197,177**
Net Adjustments	-1,920	-1,597	728	450	2,648	2,048
Total Census Basis	**-58,716**	**-61,384**	**121,398**	**133,746**	**180,113**	**195,129**
North America	-5,860	-9,023	41,607	43,515	47,467	52,539
Canada	-2,941	-3,961	22,464	24,734	25,405	28,696
Mexico	-2,918	-5,062	19,144	18,781	22,062	23,843
Europe	-10,434	-14,911	26,201	26,460	36,635	41,371
European Union	-9,323	-13,476	22,266	22,131	31,589	35,607
Austria	-39	-602	791	195	831	797
Belgium	1,513	881	2,878	2,556	1,365	1,675
Czech Republic	-205	-249	174	164	378	413
Finland	-265	-255	157	184	422	439
France	-924	-1,343	2,577	2,537	3,501	3,880
Germany	-5,298	-6,301	3,744	3,806	9,042	10,108
Hungary	-291	-326	135	164	426	490
Ireland	-2,356	-3,067	621	546	2,977	3,613
Italy	-2,021	-2,157	1,221	1,413	3,242	3,570
Netherlands	1,635	1,958	3,228	3,593	1,593	1,634
Poland	-89	-159	300	297	389	456
Spain	-127	-430	918	818	1,045	1,247
Sweden	-419	-551	295	350	714	901
United Kingdom	252	-260	4,423	4,580	4,172	4,840
Other	-689	-616	803	927	1,492	1,543
Norway	-37	-59	242	308	279	367
Russia	-926	-1,155	645	547	1,570	1,702
Switzerland	-467	-879	1,691	1,781	2,159	2,660
Other Europe	319	659	1,358	1,694	1,039	1,035
Euro Area	-8,030	-11,483	16,607	16,134	24,637	27,617
Pacific Rim Countries	-36,878	-34,184	29,618	34,908	66,496	69,092
Australia	1,098	1,037	1,975	1,985	878	947
China	-28,606	-28,053	9,552	12,166	38,158	40,219
Indonesia	-1,078	-961	580	532	1,658	1,493
Japan	-5,766	-5,651	5,117	5,777	10,883	11,427
Malaysia	-1,620	-1,666	966	1,218	2,586	2,884
Philippines	-152	-198	690	689	842	887
Newly Industrialized Countries (NICs)	-726	1,136	10,403	11,958	11,129	10,822
Hong Kong	2,497	2,887	2,863	3,294	366	407
Korea, South	-3,068	-2,049	3,318	3,839	6,386	5,888
Singapore	1,036	1,140	2,302	2,447	1,266	1,307
Taiwan	-1,192	-842	1,919	2,378	3,111	3,220
Other	-27	171	335	583	362	413
South/Central America	2,086	2,627	12,750	14,789	10,663	12,162
Argentina	324	514	687	845	363	331
Brazil	367	277	2,833	3,120	2,466	2,843
Chile	191	396	1,168	1,162	976	766
Colombia	151	264	1,379	1,906	1,228	1,642
Other	1,052	1,176	6,682	7,757	5,631	6,580
OPEC	-1,122	-1,365	5,614	7,785	6,736	9,150
Nigeria	85	6	231	389	145	382
Saudi Arabia	-628	-734	1,528	2,242	2,156	2,976
Venezuela	-885	-856	693	1,123	1,579	1,980
Other	306	219	3,162	4,030	2,856	3,811
Africa	66	-152	2,214	2,839	2,148	2,992
Algeria	-122	-178	149	222	270	400
Egypt	238	343	357	457	120	114
South Africa	-243	-323	476	521	719	844
Other	194	6	1,233	1,640	1,039	1,633
Other Countries	-7,357	-5,938	4,996	6,003	12,354	11,941
India	-2,089	-1,492	1,544	1,962	3,633	3,454
Thailand	-1,154	-1,289	1,058	1,186	2,211	2,475
Other	-4,115	-3,157	2,395	2,855	6,509	6,013
Unidentified Countries (2)	(-)	(-)	(-)	(-)	(X)	(X)

(1) Detailed data are presented on a Census basis. The information needed to convert to a BOP basis is not available.
(2) The export totals reflect shipments of certain grains, oilseeds, and satellites that are not included in the country/area totals.

NOTES:
* This exhibit is not additive; countries may be included in more than one area. For a list of countries in each area, see the information section on page A-1 of this release or at www.census.gov/ft900 or www.bea.gov/newsreleases/international/trade/tradnewsrelease.htm.
* Area data reflect the composition of the areas at yearend.
* For information on data sources, nonsampling errors, definitions, and details concerning what is included in Net Adjustments, see the informa ion section on page A-1 of this release or at www.census.gov/ft900 or www.bea.gov/newsreleases/international/trade/tradnewsrelease.htm.

Part B: NOT Seasonally Adjusted

Exhibit 15. U.S. Trade in Goods by Principal Commodities

In millions of dollars. Details may not equal totals due to rounding. This exhibit is not additive.
(R) - Revised. (X) - Not applicable. (-) Represents zero or less than one-half of measurement shown.

Item (1)	2016		2015			
	January		December		January	
	Exports	Imports	Exports	Imports	Exports	Imports
Total Balance of Payment Basis (2)	**108,892**	**167,626**	**120,543**	**181,497**	**122,126**	**182,761**
Net Adjustments (2)	439	1,778	634	1,823	728	2,648
Total Census Basis (2)	**108,453**	**165,848**	**119,909**	**179,674**	**121,398**	**180,113**
Manufactured Goods (3)	79,230	144,666	87,026	156,214	88,752	151,581
Agricultural Commodities (3)	10,099	9,435	11,228	9,443	12,290	9,511
Food and Live Animals	**6,550**	**8,465**	**7,351**	**8,449**	**7,482**	**8,514**
Live animals other than fish	37	205	84	266	43	236
Meat and preparations	1,119	757	1,244	677	1,341	892
Dairy products and birds' eggs	310	174	337	195	350	146
Fish and preparations	204	1,543	301	1,700	219	1,710
Cereals and preparations	1,496	721	1,601	761	1,875	712
Vegetables and fruit	1,505	3,095	1,753	2,810	1,527	2,869
Sugars, preparations and honey	135	355	147	327	156	341
Coffee, tea, cocoa and spices	227	1,058	255	1,074	236	1,017
Feeding stuff for animals	854	218	896	253	1,062	253
Miscellaneous edible products	663	339	735	386	673	338
Beverages and Tobacco	**439**	**1,609**	**517**	**1,822**	**436**	**1,619**
Beverages	312	1,508	372	1,670	310	1,490
Tobacco and manufactures	126	101	144	152	126	129
Crude Materials Except Fuels	**5,863**	**2,306**	**6,148**	**2,386**	**7,594**	**2,867**
Hides, skins and furskins, raw	181	21	143	17	194	32
Oil seeds and oleaginous fruits	2,310	95	2,629	81	3,333	114
Crude rubber	206	220	184	200	222	273
Cork and wood	511	552	462	530	476	559
Pulp and waste paper	716	239	696	250	730	255
Textile fibers, including waste	437	109	391	109	595	133
Crude fertilizers	192	196	199	231	191	265
Metalliferous ores and metal scrap	1,061	410	1,153	545	1,593	680
Crude animal and vegetable materials	249	463	291	423	259	555
Mineral Fuels and Lubricants	**6,719**	**11,312**	**7,817**	**12,968**	**9,622**	**19,614**
Coal, coke and briquettes	297	70	341	98	677	116
Petroleum products and preparations	5,513	10,281	6,505	12,150	7,939	18,094
Gas, natural and manufactured	896	727	959	592	983	1,202
Electric current	13	235	12	128	22	203
Animal and Vegetables Oils	**193**	**462**	**282**	**452**	**248**	**454**
Animal oils and fats	39	17	40	18	47	16
Fixed vegetable fats and oils, crude	132	432	220	419	181	425
Animal or vegetables fats, processed	22	12	22	15	20	13
Chemicals and Related Products	**15,006**	**16,261**	**14,871**	**17,558**	**16,112**	**17,078**
Organic chemicals	2,569	3,409	2,485	3,671	2,771	4,196
Inorganic chemicals	729	1,023	877	828	791	968
Dyeing, tanning and coloring materials	518	284	522	282	587	301
Medicinial and pharmaceutical products	4,179	6,983	3,644	7,973	4,399	6,625
Essen ial oils and resinoids	1,160	1,037	1,217	1,198	1,142	1,013
Fertilizers	207	474	320	538	275	698
Plastics in primary forms	2,473	1,123	2,497	1,049	2,685	1,249
Plastics in nonprimary forms	973	725	982	728	1,018	794
Chemical materials and products	2,197	1,204	2,326	1,292	2,444	1,233

Part B: NOT Seasonally Adjusted

Exhibit 15. U.S. Trade in Goods by Principal Commodities

In millions of dollars. Details may not equal totals due to rounding. This exhibit is not additive.
(R) - Revised. (X) - Not applicable. (-) Represents zero or less than one-half of measurement shown.

Item (1)	2016		2015			
	January		December		January	
	Exports	Imports	Exports	Imports	Exports	Imports
Manufactured Goods by Material	**8,096**	**18,331**	**7,925**	**17,697**	**9,061**	**21,634**
Leather and lea her manufactures	86	108	85	115	92	108
Rubber manufactures (4)	635	1,595	653	1,671	718	1,659
Cork and wood manufactures	144	812	159	785	160	778
Paper and paperboard	1,171	1,263	1,174	1,201	1,256	1,287
Textile yarn, fabrics	954	2,196	889	2,129	1,029	2,175
Nonmetallic mineral manufactures (4)	1,007	3,688	1,039	3,352	1,014	3,654
Iron and steel	1,073	2,247	1,008	2,121	1,456	4,618
Nonferrous metals	1,066	2,484	986	2,412	1,225	3,467
Manufactures of metals	1,959	3,937	1,932	3,910	2,110	3,887
Machinery and Transport Equipment	**35,748**	**71,116**	**41,282**	**81,524**	**39,395**	**72,791**
Power generating machinery (4)	2,727	5,012	3,121	5,405	3,185	5,114
Specialized industrial machinery	2,893	3,291	3,066	3,718	3,594	3,989
Metalworking machinery	370	676	451	817	439	773
General industrial machinery	4,781	7,102	5,018	7,072	5,307	7,460
Office machines	1,571	8,159	1,802	9,552	1,753	8,972
Telecommunications equipment (4)	1,571	10,905	1,889	13,441	1,968	11,649
Electrical machinery (4)	6,338	12,637	6,521	13,182	6,544	12,396
Road vehicles	7,451	21,159	8,473	24,321	7,687	19,638
Transport equipment (4)	8,045	2,175	10,941	4,016	8,919	2,800
Miscellaneous Manufactured Articles	**8,888**	**28,810**	**9,828**	**28,845**	**9,269**	**27,778**
Prefabricated buildings	189	1,058	206	1,041	214	960
Furniture (4)	488	3,992	501	3,850	510	3,591
Travel goods	48	873	55	867	39	886
Apparel and clothing accessories	242	7,291	263	6,819	256	7,218
Footwear	57	2,420	67	2,028	60	2,283
Scientific and controlling equipment (4)	3,595	3,801	4,190	4,561	3,887	3,861
Photographic equipment	468	1,116	503	1,185	499	1,183
Miscellaneous manufactured articles	3,801	8,259	4,043	8,494	3,804	7,796
Miscellaneous Commodities	**4,363**	**7,176**	**5,103**	**8,127**	**5,229**	**7,064**
Special transactions	611	5,000	799	5,545	606	5,220
Coin, including gold coin	48	147	43	196	47	95
Coin, other than gold	2	1	2	3	3	1
Gold, nonmonetary	1,263	740	1,631	978	1,892	964
Low value estimate	2,440	1,288	2,628	1,404	2,680	782
Re-Exports	**16,588**	**(X)**	**18,786**	**(X)**	**17,099**	**(X)**
Manufactured Goods (3)	15,793	(X)	17,422	(X)	16,192	(X)
Agricultural Commodities (3)	447	(X)	381	(X)	440	(X)

(1) Detailed data are presented for domestic exports unless o herwise noted. All data are on a Census basis. The information needed to convert to a BOP basis is not available.
(2) Total exports including re-exports (exports of foreign merchandise).
(3) Manufactured Goods is based on the North American Industry Classification System (NAICS) and Agricultural Commodities is based on the Harmonized System commodities specified by the U.S. Department of Agriculture definition. All other commodity detail is based on the Standard International Trade Classification (SITC).
(4) Export statistics for certain commodity classifications related to the aircraft industry are subject to suppression and have been aggregated in a manner that prevents the disclosure of confidential information. For additional information, see www.census.gov/foreign-trade/statistics/notices/aircraft/.

NOTE: For information on data sources, nonsampling errors, definitions, and details concerning what is included in Net Adjustments, see the information section on page A-1 of this release or at www.census.gov/ft900 or www.bea.gov/newsreleases/international/trade/tradnewsrelease.htm.

Part B: NOT Seasonally Adjusted

Exhibit 16. U.S. Trade in Advanced Technology Products

In millions of dollars. Details may not equal totals due to rounding.

Period	Balance	Exports	Imports
2014			
Jan.- Dec.	-84,969	336,370	421,338
Jan.-	-4,953	25,272	30,225
January	-4,953	25,272	30,225
February	-2,952	24,452	27,404
March	-3,872	29,341	33,213
April	-8,039	27,072	35,111
May	-7,595	27,646	35,240
June	-7,361	28,484	35,845
July	-7,100	27,115	34,214
August	-4,422	28,880	33,302
September	-10,303	28,317	38,619
October	-8,998	30,467	39,465
November	-11,446	28,213	39,659
December	-7,930	31,113	39,042
2015			
Jan.- Dec.	-91,856	342,618	434,474
Jan.-	-4,971	27,100	32,071
January	-4,971	27,100	32,071
February	-3,129	25,576	28,705
March	-6,345	29,548	35,892
April	-6,370	28,840	35,210
May	-7,233	27,526	34,758
June	-8,803	29,777	38,580
July	-7,401	27,909	35,310
August	-7,228	28,176	35,404
September	-10,814	29,404	40,218
October	-10,419	31,010	41,429
November	-11,439	28,095	39,534
December	-7,706	29,656	37,361
2016			
Jan.-	-4,979	25,465	30,444
January	-4,979	25,465	30,444
February			
March			
April			
May			
June			
July			
August			
September			
October			
November			
December			

NOTES:

* Export statistics for certain commodity classifications related to the aircraft industry are subject to suppression and have been aggregated in a manner that prevents the disclosure of confidential information. As a result, Advanced Technology Product exports are overstated by $402 million in January 2016. For additional information, see www.census.gov/foreign-trade/statistics/notices/aircraft/.

* Data are not available on a BOP basis. For information on data sources, nonsampling errors, and definitions, see the information section on page A-1 of this release or at www.census.gov/ft900 or www.bea.gov/newsreleases/international/trade/tradnewsrelease.htm.

Part B: NOT Seasonally Adjusted

Exhibit 16a. U.S. Trade in Advanced Technology Products by Technology Group and Selected Countries and Areas

In millions of dollars. Details may not equal totals due to rounding. (-) Represents zero or less than one-half of measurement shown.

Technology Group	January 2016			December 2015			Year-to-Date 2016			Year-to-Date 2015		
	Balance	Exports	Imports	Balance	Exports	Imports	Balance	Exports	Imports	Balance	Exports	Imports
Total	**-4,979**	**25,465**	**30,444**	**-7,706**	**29,656**	**37,361**	**-4,979**	**25,465**	**30,444**	**-4,971**	**27,100**	**32,071**
Advanced Materials	25	209	184	-29	161	189	25	209	184	-22	174	197
Aerospace (1)	5,418	8,780	3,362	6,247	11,526	5,279	5,418	8,780	3,362	5,773	9,603	3,830
Biotechnology	521	1,918	1,397	-86	1,284	1,371	521	1,918	1,397	589	1,714	1,126
Electronics	640	3,370	2,730	565	3,530	2,965	640	3,370	2,730	756	3,660	2,903
Flexible Manufacturing	265	1,108	844	179	1,338	1,159	265	1,108	844	197	1,227	1,029
Information and Communications (1)	-9,274	7,246	16,520	-11,663	8,433	20,096	-9,274	7,246	16,520	-10,238	7,810	18,048
Life Science	-984	2,208	3,191	-1,301	2,658	3,959	-984	2,208	3,191	-1,104	2,296	3,400
Nuclear Technology	-222	76	297	-47	79	126	-222	76	297	-51	44	95
Opto-Electronics (1)	-1,519	323	1,842	-1,744	405	2,149	-1,519	323	1,842	-967	423	1,390
Weapons	151	228	77	173	241	68	151	228	77	96	150	54

Selected Countries and Areas	January 2016			December 2015			Year-to-Date 2016			Year-to-Date 2015		
	Balance	Exports	Imports	Balance	Exports	Imports	Balance	Exports	Imports	Balance	Exports	Imports
Total	**-4,979**	**25,465**	**30,444**	**-7,706**	**29,656**	**37,361**	**-4,979**	**25,465**	**30,444**	**-4,971**	**27,100**	**32,071**
North America	410	5,261	4,851	189	6,486	6,297	410	5,261	4,851	503	5,246	4,743
Canada	1,094	1,938	844	888	2,780	1,892	1,094	1,938	844	965	2,264	1,300
Mexico	-685	3,322	4,007	-699	3,706	4,405	-685	3,322	4,007	-462	2,982	3,444
European Union	684	6,337	5,652	-106	6,703	6,810	684	6,337	5,652	608	6,490	5,881
France	18	958	940	-43	1,082	1,124	18	958	940	40	1,043	1,003
Germany	-162	999	1,161	-572	1,136	1,708	-162	999	1,161	-148	1,121	1,269
Ireland	-1,219	358	1,576	-1,336	183	1,519	-1,219	358	1,576	-1,175	188	1,363
taly	-38	297	335	44	390	346	-38	297	335	-6	282	288
United Kingdom	603	1,145	542	1,000	1,567	567	603	1,145	542	695	1,309	614
Other	1,482	2,580	1,098	801	2,346	1,545	1,482	2,580	1,098	1,202	2,547	1,345
Pacific Rim Countries	-8,497	8,523	17,020	-10,499	9,807	20,306	-8,497	8,523	17,020	-9,234	9,500	18,734
Australia	184	312	127	311	409	98	184	312	127	492	582	89
China	-8,599	2,037	10,636	-9,734	3,376	13,111	-8,599	2,037	10,636	-9,602	2,620	12,222
Indonesia	240	285	45	123	179	56	240	285	45	105	165	59
Japan	-247	1,244	1,491	-641	1,210	1,850	-247	1,244	1,491	-227	1,425	1,652
Malaysia	-1,055	532	1,588	-1,504	565	2,069	-1,055	532	1,588	-1,057	567	1,624
Philippines	-21	232	252	-49	224	273	-21	232	252	-36	282	317
Newly Industrialized Countries	934	3,802	2,867	914	3,745	2,831	934	3,802	2,867	1,010	3,766	2,756
Hong Kong	838	873	35	899	944	46	838	873	35	888	928	40
Korea, South	-202	991	1,193	-39	1,029	1,069	-202	991	1,193	-166	991	1,157
Singapore	203	775	572	338	925	587	203	775	572	477	975	498
Taiwan	94	1,162	1,068	-284	847	1,130	94	1,162	1,068	-189	871	1,060
Other	67	80	13	80	98	18	67	80	13	81	93	13
South/Central America	1,820	2,092	272	2,031	2,648	616	1,820	2,092	272	1,710	2,016	306
Brazil	491	637	146	323	758	436	491	637	146	682	808	126
Other	1,329	1,455	126	1,709	1,889	180	1,329	1,455	126	1,028	1,208	180
Other Countries	603	3,252	2,648	679	4,012	3,332	603	3,252	2,648	1,442	3,849	2,407
India	68	230	162	119	267	148	68	230	162	125	273	148
Israel	-49	246	295	-235	224	458	-49	246	295	6	318	312
Thailand	-519	232	752	-622	297	919	-519	232	752	-383	490	873
Other	1,103	2,543	1,440	1,417	3,224	1,807	1,103	2,543	1,440	1,695	2,768	1,073

(1) Export statistics for certain commodity classifications related to the aircraft industry are subject to suppression and have been aggregated in a manner that prevents the disclosure of confidential information. As a result, Advanced Technology Product exports are overstated by $402 million in January 2016. For additional information, see www.census.gov/foreign-trade/statistics/notices/aircraft/.

NOTE: Data are not available on a BOP basis. For information on data sources, nonsampling errors, and definitions, see the information section on page A-1 of this release or at www census gov/ft900 or www bea gov/newsreleases/international/trade/tradnewsrelease.htm.

Part B: NOT Seasonally Adjusted

Exhibit 17. U.S. Imports of Energy-Related Petroleum Products, Including Crude Oil

Details may not equal totals due to rounding.

Period	Total energy-related petroleum products (1)		Crude oil			
	Quantity (thousands of barrels)	Value (thousands of dollars)	Quantity (thousands of barrels)	Thousands of barrels per day (average)	Value (thousands of dollars)	Unit price (dollars)
2015						
Jan.- Dec.	3,384,807	170,164,481	2,662,052	7,293	125,819,431	47.26
Jan.-	292,867	17,679,621	222,776	7,186	13,133,885	58.96
January	292,867	17,679,621	222,776	7,186	13,133,885	58.96
February	250,650	13,266,616	192,052	6,859	9,511,905	49.53
March	286,647	14,371,141	226,375	7,302	10,520,000	46.47
April	294,595	14,881,910	235,934	7,864	10,975,603	46.52
May	265,139	14,789,361	201,878	6,512	10,246,955	50.76
June	287,135	16,483,337	223,390	7,446	12,009,050	53.76
July	300,035	17,235,613	236,579	7,632	12,822,942	54.20
August	279,613	14,537,472	219,426	7,078	10,823,848	49.33
September	293,965	13,300,452	231,423	7,714	9,887,183	42.72
October	262,938	11,115,676	206,740	6,669	8,293,843	40.12
November	261,869	10,723,821	211,053	7,035	8,282,101	39.24
December	309,354	11,779,461	254,425	8,207	9,312,116	36.60
2016						
Jan.-	292,271	9,827,126	226,665	7,312	7,266,196	32.06
January	292,271	9,827,126	226,665	7,312	7,266,196	32.06
February						
March						
April						
May						
June						
July						
August						
September						
October						
November						
December						

(1) Details shown for Energy-Related Petroleum Products are not available on a BOP basis. These products include the following SITC commodity groupings: crude oil, petroleum preparations, and liquefied propane and butane gas.

NOTE: For information on data sources, nonsampling errors, and definitions, see the information section on page A-1 of this release or at www.census.gov/ft900 or www.bea.gov/newsreleases/international/trade/tradnewsrelease.htm.

Part B: NOT Seasonally Adjusted

Exhibit 17a. U.S. Imports of Crude Oil by Selected Countries

Details may not equal totals due to rounding. (-) Represents zero or less than one-half unit of measurement shown.

Country	Quantity (thousands of barrels)		Customs Value (thousands of dollars)		C.I.F. Value (thousands of dollars)	
	January 2016	December 2015	January 2016	December 2015	January 2016	December 2015
Total	**226,665**	**254,425**	**7,266,196**	**9,312,116**	**7,807,745**	**9,941,711**
OPEC	87,582	106,040	3,000,336	4,148,315	3,221,037	4,431,808
Algeria	(-)	(-)	(-)	(-)	(-)	(-)
Angola	4,633	4,341	186,195	192,851	197,076	200,324
Ecuador	10,316	6,712	300,522	257,762	327,887	272,551
Indonesia (1)	1,979	1,348	76,534	60,672	84,396	64,634
Iran	(-)	(-)	(-)	(-)	(-)	(-)
Iraq	5,051	16,617	201,685	644,076	214,016	687,538
Kuwait	4,882	8,213	183,760	332,635	196,996	348,649
L bya	(-)	189	(-)	9,330	(-)	9,587
Nigeria	3,063	2,683	129,726	134,097	136,815	139,633
Qatar	(-)	(-)	(-)	(-)	(-)	(-)
Saudi Arabia	37,495	40,457	1,422,338	1,708,422	1,523,923	1,842,806
United Arab Emirates	(-)	(-)	(-)	(-)	(-)	(-)
Venezuela	20,163	25,479	499,575	808,471	539,927	866,086
Non-OPEC	139,083	148,385	4,265,861	5,163,801	4,586,708	5,509,903
Argentina	1,176	482	49,468	20,881	54,544	22,707
Azerbaijan	(-)	(-)	(-)	(-)	(-)	(-)
Brazil	5,164	5,723	174,815	214,279	189,114	228,749
Canada	97,030	101,295	2,927,538	3,425,527	3,176,503	3,690,552
Chad	1,763	2,813	59,208	109,923	63,223	116,497
Colombia	12,151	11,909	369,305	458,127	392,834	481,387
Congo (Brazzaville)	201	50	7,332	1,827	7,833	1,952
Equatorial Guinea	(-)	(-)	(-)	(-)	(-)	(-)
Gabon	(-)	662	20	28,672	21	29,334
Mexico	19,600	22,854	612,191	789,107	633,583	817,035
Norway	(-)	(-)	(-)	(-)	(-)	(-)
Russia	495	1,466	20,212	69,374	21,370	73,260
United Kingdom	527	(-)	21,381	(-)	21,509	(-)
Other Non-OPEC	976	1,132	24,391	46,084	26,176	48,431

(1) Indonesia rejoined OPEC on January 1, 2016. For comparison purposes, Indonesia is included in OPEC for both the December 2015 and the January 2016 statistics in this exhibit.

NOTE: Data are not available on a BOP basis. For information on data sources, nonsampling errors, and definitions, see the information section on page A-1 of this release or at www.census.gov/ft900 or www.bea.gov/newsreleases/international/trade/tradnewsrelease.htm.

Part B: NOT Seasonally Adjusted

Exhibit 18. U.S. Trade in Motor Vehicles and Parts by Selected Countries

In millions of dollars. Details may not equal totals due to rounding. (X) Not applicable. (-) Represents zero or less than one-half of measurement shown.

Country	Total		Passenger Cars		Trucks, Buses, Special Purpose Vehicles		Parts	
	January 2016	December 2015	January 2016	December 2015	January 2016	December 2015	January 2016	December 2015
	Exports							
TOTAL	**10,426**	**11,541**	**2,915**	**3,974**	**1,184**	**1,536**	**6,327**	**6,031**
Australia	202	224	105	106	18	39	79	79
Belgium	60	68	19	21	5	9	36	38
Brazil	44	65	2	5	(-)	1	42	59
Canada	4,065	4,268	726	981	836	1,051	2,504	2,236
Chile	37	67	11	21	4	14	23	32
China	644	720	438	517	9	12	197	190
Colombia	21	34	4	10	(-)	4	17	20
France	42	47	13	15	3	1	26	32
Germany	515	506	343	354	5	5	166	148
Hong Kong	49	54	24	24	(-)	(-)	25	30
Japan	145	198	28	59	1	2	116	138
Korea, South	159	241	94	165	(-)	1	64	75
Kuwait	30	88	15	63	12	21	2	4
Mexico	2,713	2,593	279	296	109	106	2,325	2,191
Nigeria	21	27	15	21	2	2	4	4
Russia	52	45	6	11	15	7	31	27
Saudi Arabia	235	495	172	411	47	64	16	21
Singapore	22	22	(-)	(-)	(-)	(-)	22	21
South Africa	30	47	3	20	6	3	21	24
United Arab Emirates	171	299	108	225	13	26	50	48
United Kingdom	261	236	153	132	3	3	105	101
Venezuela	16	27	8	15	1	7	7	5
Other	892	1 167	348	502	95	158	449	507
	Imports							
TOTAL	**26,855**	**29,888**	**12,869**	**15,918**	**2,527**	**2,766**	**11,459**	**11,204**
Austria	132	176	46	83	(-)	1	86	92
Brazil	78	91	(-)	1	4	1	73	88
Canada	5,065	5,526	3,624	4,087	146	225	1,295	1,214
China	1,586	1,428	32	38	22	16	1,532	1,375
Germany	2,165	3,345	1,311	2,473	21	21	834	851
Italy	292	528	184	406	1	1	107	121
Japan	3,882	4,846	2,906	3,603	46	68	930	1,175
Korea, South	2,555	2,205	1,820	1,498	(-)	(-)	735	706
Mexico	8,022	8,313	1,615	2,114	2,165	2,293	4,242	3,906
South Africa	254	243	215	190	3	6	37	47
Sweden	180	266	128	218	24	23	28	26
Taiwan	275	267	3	4	(-)	1	272	262
Thailand	227	209	13	12	(-)	(-)	214	196
United Kingdom	629	750	508	614	41	35	80	102
Other	1 512	1 695	465	576	52	74	995	1 044

NOTE: Data are not available on a BOP basis. For information on data sources, nonsampling errors, and definitions, see the information section on page A-1 of this release or at www.census gov/ft900 or www.bea.gov/newsreleases/international/trade/tradnewsrelease htm.

Part C: Seasonally Adjusted (by Geography)

Exhibit 19. U.S. Trade in Goods by Selected Countries and Areas - Census Basis

In millions of dollars.

Country and Area	January 2016	December 2015	Fourth Quarter 2014	First Quarter 2015	Second Quarter 2015	Third Quarter 2015	Fourth Quarter 2015	Year-to-Date 2016	Year-to-Date 2015
Balance									
Brazil	578	212	1,750	1,813	2,181	231	34	578	689
Canada	-459	-1,374	-7,887	-3,088	-3,052	-5,986	-2,738	-459	-859
China	-31,108	-29,683	-89,752	-96,260	-87,024	-92,365	-90,045	-31,108	-30,212
France	-1,472	-1,399	-3,946	-3,788	-4,263	-4,390	-5,126	-1,472	-1,243
Germany	-5,809	-6,352	-18,403	-18,555	-19,120	-18,470	-18,048	-5,809	-6,444
India	-2,255	-1,970	-5,874	-5,981	-5,185	-5,918	-6,127	-2,255	-2,040
Italy	-2,379	-2,215	-6,535	-7,178	-6,973	-6,691	-6,914	-2,379	-2,384
Japan	-5,589	-6,264	-16,791	-17,178	-18,219	-16,076	-17,174	-5,589	-6,512
Korea, South	-2,876	-2,493	-8,034	-7,683	-6,771	-6,808	-7,067	-2,876	-3,046
Mexico	-5,565	-4,810	-15,330	-13,420	-13,758	-14,633	-16,553	-5,565	-3,833
Saudi Arabia	-194	-471	-3,835	-771	-1,105	-339	-175	-194	-400
United Kingdom	-138	563	295	-497	-1,270	-1,157	1,472	-138	-1
All other countries	-4,906	-7,563	-13,535	-12,418	-12,811	-11,091	-22,229	-4,906	-3,854
CAFTA-DR	429	313	954	967	1,303	1,432	1,465	429	459
European Union	-12,565	-13,344	-37,287	-34,434	-39,208	-40,127	-39,549	-12,565	-12,385
Newly Industrialized Countries	-778	-117	2,099	-1,705	-573	-164	226	-778	-363
OPEC (1)	-154	-228	-6,930	566	1,410	3,403	1,252	-154	-873
South/Central America	3,126	2,755	8,921	8,900	10,704	9,548	8,282	3,126	2,139
Exports									
Brazil	2,369	2,441	10,001	9,035	8,939	7,029	6,663	2,369	3,208
Canada	22,466	22,609	79,003	71,887	70,898	69,584	67,958	22,466	24,870
China	8,643	8,618	31,601	28,306	30,221	30,355	27,304	8,643	10,013
France	2,324	2,451	7,544	7,812	7,551	7,444	7,270	2,324	2,662
Germany	3,880	4,140	11,735	12,416	12,250	12,377	12,904	3,880	3,979
India	1,669	1,532	6,101	5,515	5,954	5,138	4,922	1,669	1,714
Italy	1,288	1,527	4,307	3,889	4,035	4,069	4,256	1,288	1,270
Japan	4,862	4,759	16,250	16,145	16,270	15,225	14,833	4,862	5,250
Korea, South	3,395	3,224	10,938	10,590	11,441	11,162	10,306	3,395	3,550
Mexico	19,485	19,488	59,871	58,598	59,988	59,825	57,967	19,485	20,050
Saudi Arabia	1,364	1,400	4,852	4,771	4,865	5,420	4,634	1,364	1,781
United Kingdom	4,126	4,528	13,853	13,220	14,726	13,951	14,456	4,126	4,666
All other countries	41,363	42,524	148,050	139,467	136,603	135,707	128,759	41,363	46,550
CAFTA-DR	2,345	2,228	7,496	7,089	7,182	7,324	7,306	2,345	2,501
European Union	21,552	22,062	67,661	69,861	68,015	66,628	68,184	21,552	23,368
Newly Industrialized Countries	10,620	10,823	35,977	33,188	34,793	34,028	33,249	10,620	11,037
OPEC (1)	5,795	5,207	20,936	18,601	18,079	19,345	16,755	5,795	6,186
South/Central America	11,072	11,708	45,115	40,536	40,178	37,495	35,097	11,072	13,139
Imports									
Brazil	1,791	2,229	8,251	7,222	6,757	6,797	6,629	1,791	2,519
Canada	22,925	23,982	86,890	74,975	73,949	75,570	70,696	22,925	25,729
China	39,751	38,301	121,353	124,566	117,245	122,720	117,350	39,751	40,225
France	3,796	3,850	11,490	11,600	11,814	11,834	12,396	3,796	3,905
Germany	9,689	10,493	30,138	30,971	31,370	30,847	30,951	9,689	10,423
India	3,925	3,502	11,975	11,497	11,138	11,057	11,049	3,925	3,754
Italy	3,666	3,742	10,841	11,067	11,008	10,760	11,170	3,666	3,654
Japan	10,450	11,023	33,041	33,323	34,489	31,301	32,007	10,450	11,762
Korea, South	6,271	5,718	18,971	18,273	18,212	17,970	17,372	6,271	6,596
Mexico	25,050	24,298	75,201	72,018	73,746	74,458	74,520	25,050	23,883
Saudi Arabia	1,559	1,871	8,688	5,542	5,971	5,759	4,809	1,559	2,180
United Kingdom	4,264	3,965	13,558	13,717	15,997	15,108	12,983	4,264	4,667
All other countries	46,269	50,087	161,585	151,885	149,413	146,798	150,988	46,269	50,404
CAFTA-DR	1,916	1,915	6,542	6,122	5,879	5,892	5,841	1,916	2,042
European Union	34,117	35,405	104,948	104,294	107,223	106,755	107,734	34,117	35,752
Newly Industrialized Countries	11,398	10,940	33,877	34,893	35,366	34,192	33,023	11,398	11,400
OPEC (1)	5,949	5,435	27,866	18,036	16,668	15,943	15,503	5,949	7,059
South/Central America	7,947	8,953	36,194	31,636	29,474	27,947	26,815	7,947	11,000

(1) Statistics for 2016 include Indonesia, which rejoined OPEC on January 1, 2016.

NOTES:

* Countries may be included in more than one area. For a list of countries in each area, see the information sec ion on page A-1 of this release or at www.census gov/ft900 or www.bea.gov/newsreleases/international/trade/tradnewsrelease.htm.
* Area data reflect the composi ion of the areas at the time of reporting.
* Seasonally adjusted country and area data in this exhibit will not sum to the commodity-based seasonally adjusted totals shown in Part A of this release. Data users should use caution drawing comparisons between the two sets of seasonally adjusted series.
* For information on data sources, nonsampling errors, and definitions, see the information section on page A-1 of his release or at www.census.gov/ft900 or www.bea.gov/newsreleases/international/trade/tradnewsrelease htm.

Part C: Seasonally Adjusted (by Geography)

Exhibit 20. U.S. Trade in Goods and Services by Selected Countries and Areas - BOP Basis

In millions of dollars. (R) - Revised.

Country and Area	Third Quarter 2014	Fourth Quarter 2014	First Quarter 2015 (R)	Second Quarter 2015 (R)	Third Quarter 2015 (R)	Fourth Quarter 2015	Annual 2013	Annual 2014	Annual 2015
Balance									
Brazil	7,509	6,756	7,182	7,339	5,241	4,840	35,939	32,119	24,602
Canada	-3,237	-1,420	2,188	1,751	-1,021	2,530	-4,111	-9,564	5,448
China	-79,599	-82,639	-89,925	-79,729	-85,399	-82,957	-295,604	-315,116	-338,010
France	-3,162	-3,723	-3,481	-3,934	-3,819	-4,521	-10,550	-12,873	-15,754
Germany	-20,149	-19,554	-19,452	-20,328	-19,830	-19,068	-73,162	-79,163	-78,679
India	-7,273	-6,613	-7,613	-6,724	-7,509	-7,867	-25,610	-28,481	-29,713
Italy	-7,042	-7,153	-8,059	-7,968	-7,812	-8,161	-24,045	-27,624	-31,999
Japan	-12,705	-13,636	-13,320	-15,368	-13,384	-14,682	-58,362	-53,205	-56,754
Korea, South	-3,355	-5,321	-5,128	-4,283	-3,771	-3,585	-9,360	-13,501	-16,768
Mexico	-12,627	-14,660	-12,889	-13,695	-14,228	-16,504	-47,461	-50,168	-57,316
Saudi Arabia	-3,841	-2,347	1,533	701	1,876	2,245	-25,054	-21,316	6,356
United Kingdom	4,867	3,709	2,648	1,273	1,593	4,108	7,564	12,941	9,623
All o her countries	15,163	12,584	13,463	11,947	11,525	2,273	51,420	57,626	39,208
CAFTA-DR	n.a.	n.a.	n.a.	n.a.	n.a.	n.a.	n.a.	n.a.	n.a.
European Union	-21,840	-24,291	-24,040	-29,751	-30,850	-29,035	-83,664	-92,902	-113,676
Newly Industrialized Countries	8,103	7,891	3,475	5,360	7,090	7,748	41,005	35,870	23,673
OPEC	-5,184	-1,549	6,608	6,653	9,009	7,674	-49,110	-29,615	29,944
Sou h/Central America	15,023	15,599	16,339	16,937	15,680	13,883	51,400	59,221	62,839
Exports									
Brazil	17,408	17,136	16,177	15,944	13,824	13,427	70,774	70,661	59,372
Canada	95,742	94,568	86,708	85,479	83,899	82,311	364,967	374,864	338,397
China	41,476	42,748	39,592	42,175	41,737	38,744	160,140	167,207	162,248
France	12,702	12,324	12,616	12,328	12,420	12,095	51,242	51,328	49,459
Germany	19,549	19,047	19,795	19,296	19,312	19,776	75,175	77,823	78,179
India	9,399	10,778	9,521	10,194	9,690	9,536	35,740	37,723	38,941
Italy	6,309	6,449	5,880	6,028	5,886	6,133	25,840	25,748	23,927
Japan	29,052	28,114	27,780	27,520	26,295	25,627	112,982	114,712	107,221
Korea, South	16,512	16,388	16,137	16,939	17,155	16,606	64,503	66,788	66,837
Mexico	68,352	67,532	66,551	67,812	67,501	65,416	256,554	270,721	267,280
Saudi Arabia	6,905	6,680	7,423	6,991	7,996	7,378	28,200	27,166	29,787
United Kingdom	30,696	30,311	29,324	30,263	29,570	30,183	109,173	118,145	119,340
All o her countries	235,270	233,829	226,582	222,923	219,233	213,893	924,647	940,320	882,631
CAFTA-DR	n.a.	n.a.	n.a.	n.a.	n.a.	n.a.	n.a.	n.a.	n.a.
European Union	126,002	124,703	125,116	122,436	120,003	122,330	471,467	498,394	489,886
Newly Industrialized Countries	49,238	50,189	47,370	49,697	50,056	49,563	196,931	200,703	196,686
OPEC	29,189	28,216	27,505	26,474	27,585	25,389	114,559	113,408	106,953
Sou h/Central America	71,574	70,837	67,626	66,273	62,929	59,985	286,614	286,234	256,813
Imports									
Brazil	9,899	10,379	8,995	8,605	8,583	8,588	34,836	38,542	34,770
Canada	98,980	95,988	84,521	83,728	84,920	79,781	369,078	384,428	332,949
China	121,075	125,387	129,517	121,904	127,137	121,700	455,743	482,323	500,258
France	15,864	16,047	16,096	16,262	16,238	16,616	61,792	64,200	65,213
Germany	39,698	38,602	39,247	39,625	39,142	38,844	148,337	156,986	156,858
India	16,672	17,391	17,134	16,918	17,199	17,403	61,350	66,204	68,654
Italy	13,350	13,602	13,938	13,996	13,699	14,293	49,884	53,372	55,926
Japan	41,756	41,750	41,099	42,888	39,679	40,309	171,343	167,916	163,975
Korea, South	19,867	21,709	21,266	21,222	20,926	20,191	73,863	80,290	83,604
Mexico	80,979	82,192	79,440	81,507	81,729	81,921	304,015	320,889	324,596
Saudi Arabia	10,746	9,027	5,889	6,289	6,120	5,133	53,254	48,482	23,432
United Kingdom	25,829	26,602	26,676	28,989	27,977	26,075	101,609	105,203	109,717
All o her countries	220,107	221,245	213,119	210,976	207,708	211,620	873,227	882,693	843,423
CAFTA-DR	n.a.	n.a.	n.a.	n.a.	n.a.	n.a.	n.a.	n.a.	n.a.
European Union	147,843	148,994	149,157	152,187	150,852	151,365	555,130	591,296	603,561
Newly Industrialized Countries	41,135	42,298	43,895	44,337	42,966	41,816	155,926	164,833	173,014
OPEC	34,373	29,765	20,897	19,821	18,576	17,715	163,668	143,023	77,010
Sou h/Central America	56,551	55,238	51,287	49,337	47,248	46,103	235,214	227,014	193,975

n.a. Not available

NOTES:

* Countries may be included in more than one area. For a list of countries in each area and for additional information on country and area detail for goods on a BOP basis and for services, see the information section on page A-1 of this release or at www.census.gov/ft900 or www.bea.gov/newsreleases/international/trade/tradnewsrelease.htm.
* Area data reflect the composition of the areas as they were at the time of reporting.
* Seasonally adjusted country and area data in this exhibit will not sum to the seasonally adjusted totals shown in Part A of this release. Data users should use caution drawing comparisons between he two sets of seasonally adjusted series.
* For information on data sources, nonsampling errors, and definitions, see the information section on page A-1 of this release or at www.census.gov/ft900 or www bea.gov/newsreleases/international/trade/tradnewsrelease.htm.

Part C: Seasonally Adjusted (by Geography)

Exhibit 20a. U.S. Trade in Goods by Selected Countries and Areas - BOP Basis

In millions of dollars. (R) - Revised.

Country and Area	Third Quarter 2014	Fourth Quarter 2014	First Quarter 2015 (R)	Second Quarter 2015 (R)	Third Quarter 2015 (R)	Fourth Quarter 2015	Annual 2013	Annual 2014	Annual 2015
Balance									
Brazil	2,627	1,916	2,045	2,483	424	302	16,830	12,311	5,254
Canada	-11,025	-9,291	-5,062	-5,102	-7,455	-4,032	-36,192	-40,843	-21,651
China	-86,523	-89,805	-97,133	-87,684	-92,644	-90,094	-318,794	-343,193	-367,554
France	-3,782	-4,022	-3,926	-4,479	-4,360	-5,209	-14,526	-15,922	-17,974
Germany	-19,025	-18,563	-18,967	-19,460	-18,667	-18,203	-67,608	-74,537	-75,297
India	-5,827	-5,254	-5,986	-5,181	-5,884	-6,173	-19,784	-22,889	-23,223
Italy	-6,408	-6,590	-7,359	-7,044	-6,737	-7,168	-22,213	-25,328	-28,307
Japan	-16,566	-17,167	-17,763	-18,701	-16,459	-17,904	-74,773	-68,665	-70,827
Korea, South	-5,714	-7,815	-7,518	-6,757	-6,791	-7,026	-19,521	-23,732	-28,092
Mexico	-15,293	-17,185	-15,598	-16,071	-16,350	-18,474	-59,965	-60,682	-66,493
Saudi Arabia	-6,035	-4,180	-930	-1,257	-299	-36	-33,119	-29,258	-2,521
United Kingdom	1,180	202	-581	-1,321	-1,267	1,365	-5,487	-892	-1,804
All other countries	-11,568	-13,967	-12,866	-13,222	-12,951	-21,780	-47,434	-47,830	-60,819
CAFTA-DR	913	870	897	1,207	1,363	1,376	-828	2,422	4,843
European Union	-35,263	-36,833	-35,854	-40,642	-40,382	-39,466	-127,032	-143,453	-156,343
Newly Industrialized Countries	2,038	2,328	-1,562	-720	45	494	18,404	11,962	-1,744
OPEC	-10,857	-6,804	710	1,197	2,964	1,698	-70,801	-51,825	6,570
Sou h/Central America	8,998	8,980	8,981	10,828	9,652	8,407	25,630	33,207	37,868
Exports									
Brazil	10,278	10,015	8,960	8,944	6,971	6,652	44,050	42,412	31,527
Canada	80,416	79,233	72,064	71,091	69,823	68,107	302,194	313,510	281,086
China	30,907	31,834	28,516	30,384	30,487	27,429	122,827	124,747	116,817
France	7,928	7,614	7,857	7,631	7,606	7,287	32,089	31,684	30,381
Germany	12,527	11,780	12,436	12,312	12,402	12,897	47,724	49,637	50,048
India	5,525	6,759	5,596	6,011	5,219	4,893	22,195	22,523	21,718
Italy	4,282	4,322	3,906	4,095	4,079	4,268	16,898	17,123	16,348
Japan	17,453	16,591	16,400	16,548	15,779	14,975	66,538	68,014	63,702
Korea, South	11,565	11,206	10,918	11,750	11,364	10,385	43,504	46,114	44,417
Mexico	60,817	59,956	58,688	60,025	59,899	57,862	226,766	240,721	236,473
Saudi Arabia	4,368	4,530	4,634	4,731	5,473	4,789	18,773	17,866	19,628
United Kingdom	14,712	13,985	13,330	14,892	14,025	14,536	48,395	54,547	56,782
All other countries	151,141	148,618	140,848	138,271	135,329	130,079	600,091	603,740	544,528
CAFTA-DR	7,886	7,484	7,082	7,180	7,327	7,276	29,648	31,121	28,865
European Union	70,855	68,553	70,192	68,638	67,112	68,681	265,603	279,127	274,623
Newly Industrialized Countries	35,407	36,335	33,822	35,281	34,570	33,607	143,568	145,309	137,279
OPEC	21,020	20,477	19,116	18,480	18,923	16,797	83,122	81,372	73,315
Sou h/Central America	46,768	45,295	40,532	40,293	37,588	35,173	185,064	184,680	153,585
Imports									
Brazil	7,651	8,099	6,915	6,461	6,547	6,350	27,220	30,102	26,273
Canada	91,441	88,524	77,127	76,193	77,278	72,139	338,386	354,354	302,737
China	117,430	121,640	125,649	118,068	123,130	117,523	441,621	467,940	484,371
France	11,710	11,636	11,784	12,109	11,965	12,496	46,615	47,606	48,354
Germany	31,552	30,344	31,403	31,772	31,069	31,100	115,332	124,174	125,344
India	11,353	12,014	11,582	11,191	11,102	11,066	41,979	45,412	44,942
Italy	10,690	10,912	11,265	11,138	10,816	11,436	39,111	42,451	44,655
Japan	34,019	33,758	34,163	35,249	32,238	32,879	141,312	136,680	134,528
Korea, South	17,278	19,020	18,436	18,506	18,156	17,410	63,025	69,846	72,508
Mexico	76,110	77,142	74,286	76,096	76,248	76,336	286,731	301,403	302,966
Saudi Arabia	10,403	8,710	5,564	5,988	5,772	4,825	51,892	47,125	22,149
United Kingdom	13,532	13,783	13,910	16,213	15,291	13,172	53,882	55,439	58,586
All other countries	162,710	162,584	153,714	151,492	148,281	151,859	647,526	651,570	605,346
CAFTA-DR	6,973	6,613	6,185	5,973	5,964	5,900	30,476	28,700	24,021
European Union	106,118	105,386	106,045	109,280	107,494	108,147	392,635	422,580	430,966
Newly Industrialized Countries	33,370	34,007	35,384	36,001	34,525	33,113	125,164	133,347	139,023
OPEC	31,876	27,280	18,405	17,284	15,958	15,098	153,923	133,198	66,745
Sou h/Central America	37,770	36,314	31,551	29,465	27,935	26,766	159,433	151,473	115,717

NOTES:

* Countries may be included in more than one area. For a list of countries in each area and for additional information on country and area detail for goods on a BOP basis and for services, see the information section on page A-1 of this release or at www.census.gov/ft900 or www.bea.gov/newsreleases/international/trade/tradnewsrelease.htm.
* Area data reflect the composition of the areas as they were at the time of reporting.
* Seasonally adjusted country and area data in this exhibit will not sum to the seasonally adjusted totals shown in Part A of this release. Data users should use caution drawing comparisons between he two sets of seasonally adjusted series.
* For information on data sources, nonsampling errors, and definitions, see the information section on page A-1 of this release or at www.census.gov/ft900 or www bea.gov/newsreleases/international/trade/tradnewsrelease.htm.

Part C: Seasonally Adjusted (by Geography)

Exhibit 20b. U.S. Trade in Services by Selected Countries and Areas

In millions of dollars. (R) - Revised.

Country and Area	Third Quarter 2014	Fourth Quarter 2014	First Quarter 2015 (R)	Second Quarter 2015 (R)	Third Quarter 2015 (R)	Fourth Quarter 2015	Annual 2013	Annual 2014	Annual 2015
Balance									
Brazil	4,882	4,840	5,137	4,857	4,817	4,538	19,109	19,809	19,348
Canada	7,787	7,872	7,250	6,853	6,434	6,562	32,082	31,279	27,099
China	6,924	7,166	7,208	7,955	7,244	7,137	23,190	28,077	29,545
France	620	299	446	545	541	688	3,976	3,049	2,220
Germany	-1,124	-991	-485	-869	-1,163	-865	-5,555	-4,626	-3,382
India	-1,446	-1,359	-1,627	-1,543	-1,625	-1,694	-5,825	-5,592	-6,490
Italy	-633	-563	-700	-924	-1,075	-993	-1,832	-2,296	-3,692
Japan	3,861	3,531	4,444	3,332	3,075	3,221	16,412	15,461	14,073
Korea, South	2,359	2,494	2,390	2,474	3,020	3,441	10,161	10,231	11,324
Mexico	2,665	2,525	2,709	2,376	2,122	1,970	12,504	10,514	9,177
Saudi Arabia	2,194	1,833	2,463	1,958	2,174	2,281	8,064	7,942	8,877
United Kingdom	3,687	3,507	3,229	2,595	2,860	2,744	13,052	13,834	11,427
All o her countries	26,731	26,550	26,329	25,169	24,476	24,052	98,855	105,456	100,026
CAFTA-DR	n.a.	n.a.	n.a.	n.a.	n.a.	n.a.	n.a.	n.a.	n.a.
European Union	13,422	12,543	11,814	10,891	9,532	10,431	43,368	50,550	42,667
Newly Industrialized Countries	6,065	5,563	5,037	6,080	7,046	7,254	22,601	23,908	25,417
OPEC	5,673	5,255	5,897	5,456	6,045	5,976	21,691	22,210	23,374
Sou h/Central America	6,025	6,618	7,358	6,109	6,028	5,476	25,770	26,014	24,970
Exports									
Brazil	7,130	7,120	7,217	7,000	6,853	6,775	26,725	28,249	27,845
Canada	15,326	15,335	14,644	14,388	14,076	14,204	62,773	61,353	57,311
China	10,569	10,914	11,075	11,791	11,251	11,315	37,313	42,460	45,431
France	4,774	4,710	4,758	4,698	4,814	4,808	19,153	19,643	19,078
Germany	7,022	7,267	7,359	6,984	6,910	6,878	27,451	28,186	28,131
India	3,874	4,019	3,925	4,184	4,471	4,642	13,546	15,200	17,222
Italy	2,027	2,127	1,974	1,933	1,807	1,865	8,942	8,625	7,579
Japan	11,599	11,523	11,379	10,972	10,516	10,652	46,444	46,698	43,519
Korea, South	4,947	5,182	5,219	5,189	5,790	6,221	20,999	20,675	22,420
Mexico	7,535	7,576	7,863	7,787	7,603	7,554	29,788	30,000	30,807
Saudi Arabia	2,537	2,150	2,788	2,260	2,523	2,588	9,427	9,299	10,159
United Kingdom	15,984	16,326	15,995	15,371	15,545	15,647	60,779	63,597	62,558
All other countries	84,129	85,211	85,734	84,652	83,903	83,813	324,556	336,580	338,103
CAFTA-DR	n.a.	n.a.	n.a.	n.a.	n.a.	n.a.	n.a.	n.a.	n.a.
European Union	55,147	56,150	54,925	53,798	52,891	53,649	205,863	219,266	215,263
Newly Industrialized Countries	13,831	13,854	13,548	14,416	15,486	15,957	53,363	55,394	59,407
OPEC	8,170	7,739	8,389	7,994	8,663	8,592	31,436	32,036	33,638
Sou h/Central America	24,806	25,542	27,094	25,981	25,341	24,812	101,550	101,554	103,228
Imports									
Brazil	2,247	2,281	2,080	2,144	2,035	2,237	7,616	8,440	8,497
Canada	7,539	7,464	7,394	7,535	7,642	7,642	30,692	30,074	30,213
China	3,645	3,747	3,867	3,836	4,006	4,177	14,123	14,383	15,887
France	4,153	4,411	4,313	4,153	4,273	4,120	15,177	16,594	16,859
Germany	8,146	8,258	7,845	7,852	8,073	7,744	33,006	32,812	31,513
India	5,320	5,377	5,551	5,727	6,097	6,336	19,371	20,792	23,712
Italy	2,661	2,691	2,674	2,857	2,882	2,857	10,773	10,921	11,271
Japan	7,737	7,992	6,936	7,640	7,441	7,430	30,032	31,237	29,447
Korea, South	2,588	2,688	2,830	2,716	2,770	2,780	10,838	10,444	11,096
Mexico	4,869	5,051	5,154	5,411	5,481	5,585	17,284	19,487	21,630
Saudi Arabia	343	317	326	301	348	307	1,363	1,357	1,282
United Kingdom	12,297	12,818	12,766	12,777	12,686	12,903	47,727	49,764	51,131
All o her countries	57,398	58,661	59,405	59,483	59,427	59,761	225,701	231,124	238,077
CAFTA-DR	n.a.	n a.	n.a.	n.a.	n.a.	n.a.	n.a.	n.a.	n.a.
European Union	41,725	43,608	43,111	42,907	43,358	43,218	162,496	168,716	172,596
Newly Industrialized Countries	7,766	8,291	8,511	8,336	8,441	8,703	30,762	31,487	33,990
OPEC	2,497	2,485	2,492	2,538	2,618	2,616	9,745	9,825	10,264
Sou h/Central America	18,780	18,924	19,736	19,872	19,313	19,336	75,781	75,540	78,258

n.a. Not available

NOTES:

* Countries may be included in more than one area. For a list of countries in each area and for additional information on country and area detail for goods on a BOP basis and for services, see the information section on page A-1 of this release or at www.census.gov/ft900 or www.bea.gov/newsreleases/international/trade/tradnewsrelease.htm.

* Area data reflect the composition of the areas as they were at the time of reporting.

* Seasonally adjusted country and area data in this exhibit will not sum to the seasonally adjusted totals shown in Part A of this release. Data users should use caution drawing comparisons between he two sets of seasonally adjusted series.

* For information on data sources, nonsampling errors, and definitions, see the information section on page A-1 of this release or at www.census.gov/ft900 or www bea.gov/newsreleases/international/trade/tradnewsrelease.htm.

INFORMATION ON GOODS AND SERVICES

GOODS (CENSUS BASIS)

Data for goods on a Census basis are compiled from the documents collected by the U.S. Customs and Border Protection and reflect the movement of goods between foreign countries and the 50 states, the District of Columbia, Puerto Rico, the U.S. Virgin Islands, and U.S. Foreign Trade Zones. They include government and non-government shipments of goods and exclude shipments between the United States and its territories and possessions; transactions with U.S. military, diplomatic, and consular installations abroad; U.S. goods returned to the United States by its Armed Forces; personal and household effects of travelers; and in-transit shipments. The General Imports value reflects the total arrival of merchandise from foreign countries that immediately enters consumption channels, warehouses, or Foreign Trade Zones.

For imports, the value reported is the U.S. Customs and Border Protection appraised value of merchandise—generally, the price paid for merchandise for export to the United States. Import duties, freight, insurance, and other charges incurred in bringing merchandise to the United States are excluded. The exception is Exhibit 17a, which shows CIF import value. The CIF (cost, insurance, and freight) value represents the landed value of the merchandise at the first port of arrival in the United States. It is computed by adding import charges to the customs value and therefore excludes U.S. import duties.

Exports are valued at the f.a.s. (free alongside ship) value of merchandise at the U.S. port of export, based on the transaction price including inland freight, insurance, and other charges incurred in placing the merchandise alongside the carrier at the U.S. port of exportation.

REVISION PROCEDURE (CENSUS BASIS)

Monthly Revisions: Monthly data include actual month's transactions as well as a small number of transactions for previous months. Each month, the U.S. Census Bureau revises the aggregate seasonally adjusted (current and real chained-dollar) and unadjusted export, import, and trade balance figures, as well as the end-use totals for the prior month. Country detail data and commodity detail data, based on the Standard International Trade Classification (SITC) Revision 4 and the North American Industry Classification System (NAICS), are not revised monthly. The timing adjustment shown in Exhibit 14 is the difference between monthly data as originally reported and as recompiled.

For December, unadjusted exports of goods were revised downward less than $0.1 billion and unadjusted imports of goods were revised downward $0.2 billion. Goods carry-over in January was $0.1 billion (0.1 percent) for exports and $0.4 billion (0.2 percent) for imports. For December, revised export carry-over was less than $0.1 billion (less than 0.1 percent) and revised import carry-over was less than $0.1 billion (less than 0.1 percent).

Quarterly Revisions to Chain-Weighted Dollar Series*:* For March, June, September, and December statistical month releases, revisions are made to the real chained-dollar series presented in Exhibits 10 and 11: the previous five months are revised to incorporate the Bureau of Labor Statistics' revisions to price indexes, which are used to produce the real chained-dollar series and to align Census data with data published by the U.S. Bureau of Economic Analysis (BEA) in the National Income and Product Accounts (NIPAs).

Annual Revisions*:* Each June, not seasonally adjusted goods data are revised to redistribute monthly data that arrived too late for inclusion in the month of transaction. In addition, revisions are made to reflect corrections received subsequent to the monthly revisions. Seasonally adjusted data are also revised to reflect recalculated seasonal and trading-day adjustments. These revisions are reflected in totals, end-use, commodity, and country summary data.

Other Revisions*:* For December and January statistical month releases, each prior month of the most recent full year is revised so that the totals of the seasonally adjusted months equal the annual totals.

U.S./CANADA DATA EXCHANGE AND SUBSTITUTION

Data for U.S. exports to Canada are derived from import data compiled by Canada. The use of Canada's import data to produce U.S. export data requires several alignments in order to compare the two series.

1. *Coverage* - Canadian imports are based on country of origin. U.S. goods shipped from a third country are included. U.S. exports exclude these foreign shipments. For January 2016, these shipments totaled $202.4 million. U.S. export coverage also excludes U.S. postal shipments to Canada. For January 2016, these shipments totaled $14.8 million.

   U.S. import coverage includes shipments of railcars and locomotives from Canada. Effective with January 2004 statistics, Canada excludes these shipments from its goods exports to the United States, therefore creating coverage differences between the two countries for these goods.

2. *Valuation* - Canadian imports are valued at the point of origin in the United States. However, U.S. exports are valued at the port of exit in the United States and include inland freight charges, making the U.S. export value slightly larger than the Canadian import value. Canada requires inland freight to be reported separately from the value of the goods. Combining the inland freight and the Canadian reported import value provides a consistent valuation for all U.S. exports. Inland freight charges for January 2016 accounted for 2.0 percent of the value of U.S. exports to Canada.

3. *Re-exports* - Unlike Canadian imports, which are based on country of origin, U.S. exports include re-exports of foreign goods. Therefore, the aggregate U.S. export figure is slightly larger than the Canadian import figure. For January 2016, re-exports to Canada were $3,467.7 million.

4. *Exchange Rate* - Average monthly exchange rates are applied to convert the published data to U.S. currency. For January 2016, the average exchange rate was 1.4208 Canadian dollars per U.S. dollar.

5. *Other* - There are other minor differences, such as rounding error, that are statistically insignificant.

Canadian Estimates: Effective with January 2001 statistics, the current month data for exports to Canada contain an estimate for late arrivals and corrections. In the following month, this estimate is replaced, in the news release exhibits only, with the actual value of late receipts and corrections. This estimate improves the current month data for exports to Canada and treats late receipts for exports to Canada in a manner that is more consistent with the treatment of late receipts for exports to other countries.

NONSAMPLING ERRORS

The goods data are a complete enumeration of documents collected by the U.S. Customs and Border Protection and are not subject to sampling errors. Quality assurance procedures are performed at every stage of collection, processing, and tabulation. However, the data are still subject to several types of nonsampling errors. The most significant of these include reporting errors, undocumented shipments, timeliness, data capture errors, and errors in the estimation of low-valued transactions.

Reporting Errors: Reporting errors are mistakes or omissions made by importers, exporters, or their agents in their import or export declarations. Most errors involve missing or invalid commodity classification codes and missing or incorrect quantities or shipping weights. They have a negligible effect on aggregate import, export, and balance of trade statistics. However, they can affect the detailed commodity statistics.

Undocumented Shipments: Federal regulations require importers, exporters, or their agents to report all merchandise shipments above established exemption levels. The U.S. Census Bureau has determined that not all required documents are filed, particularly for exports.

Timeliness and Data Capture Errors: The U.S. Census Bureau captures import and export information from administrative documents and through various automated collection programs. Documents may be lost, and data may be incorrectly keyed, coded, or recorded. Transactions may be included in a subsequent month's statistics if received late.

Low-valued Transactions: The total values of transactions valued as much as or below $2,500 for exports and $2,000 ($250 for certain quota items) for imports are estimated for each country, using factors based on the ratios of low-valued shipments to individual country totals for past periods.

The U.S. Census Bureau recommends that data users incorporate this information into their analyses, as nonsampling errors could impact the conclusion drawn from the results. For a detailed discussion of errors affecting the goods data, see "U.S. Merchandise Trade Statistics: A Quality Profile," available at www.census.gov/foreign-trade/aip/quality_profile10032014.pdf or from the U.S. Census Bureau, Economic Indicators Division.

AREA GROUPINGS

North America: Canada, Mexico.

Dominican Republic-Central America-United States Free Trade Agreement (CAFTA-DR): Costa Rica, Dominican Republic, El Salvador, Guatemala, Honduras, Nicaragua.

Europe: Albania, Andorra, Armenia, Austria, Azerbaijan, Belarus, Belgium, Bosnia and Herzegovina, Bulgaria, Croatia, Cyprus, Czech Republic, Denmark, Estonia, Faroe Islands, Finland, France, Georgia, Germany, Gibraltar, Greece, Hungary, Iceland, Ireland, Italy, Kazakhstan, Kosovo, Kyrgyzstan, Latvia, Liechtenstein, Lithuania, Luxembourg, Macedonia, Malta, Moldova, Monaco, Montenegro, Netherlands, Norway, Poland, Portugal, Romania, Russia, San Marino, Serbia, Slovakia, Slovenia, Spain, Svalbard-Jan Mayen Island, Sweden, Switzerland, Tajikistan, Turkey, Turkmenistan, Ukraine, United Kingdom, Uzbekistan, Vatican City.

European Union: Austria, Belgium, Bulgaria, Croatia, Cyprus, Czech Republic, Denmark, Estonia, Finland, France, Germany, Greece, Hungary, Ireland, Italy, Latvia, Lithuania, Luxembourg, Malta, Netherlands, Poland, Portugal, Romania, Slovakia, Slovenia, Spain, Sweden, United Kingdom.

Euro Area: Austria, Belgium, Cyprus, Estonia, Finland, France, Germany, Greece, Ireland, Italy, Latvia, Lithuania, Luxembourg, Malta, Netherlands, Portugal, Slovakia, Slovenia, Spain.

Newly Industrialized Countries (NICs): Hong Kong, Korea (South), Singapore, Taiwan.

Pacific Rim: Australia, Brunei, China, Hong Kong, Indonesia, Japan, Korea (South), Macau, Malaysia, New Zealand, Papua New Guinea, Philippines, Singapore, Taiwan.

South/Central America: Anguilla, Antigua and Barbuda, Argentina, Aruba, Bahamas, Barbados, Belize, Bermuda, Bolivia, Brazil, British Virgin Islands, Cayman Islands, Chile, Colombia, Costa Rica, Cuba, Curacao, Dominica, Dominican Republic, Ecuador, El Salvador, Falkland Islands (Islas Malvinas), French Guiana, Grenada, Guadeloupe, Guatemala, Guyana, Haiti, Honduras, Jamaica, Martinique, Montserrat, Netherlands Antilles, Nicaragua, Panama, Paraguay, Peru, Sint Maarten, St. Kitts and Nevis, St. Lucia, St. Vincent and the Grenadines, Suriname, Trinidad and Tobago, Turks and Caicos Islands, Uruguay, Venezuela.

Organization of Petroleum Exporting Countries (OPEC): Algeria, Angola, Ecuador, Indonesia, Iran, Iraq, Kuwait, Libya, Nigeria, Qatar, Saudi Arabia, United Arab Emirates, Venezuela.

Africa: Algeria, Angola, Benin, Botswana, British Indian Ocean Territories, Burkina Faso, Burundi, Cabo Verde, Cameroon, Central African Republic, Chad, Comoros, Congo (Brazzaville), Congo (Kinshasa), Djibouti, Egypt, Equatorial Guinea, Eritrea, Ethiopia, French Southern and Antarctic Lands, Gabon, Gambia, Ghana, Guinea, Guinea-Bissau, Ivory Coast, Kenya, Lesotho, Liberia, Libya, Madagascar, Malawi, Mali, Mauritania, Mauritius, Mayotte, Morocco, Mozambique, Namibia, Niger, Nigeria, Reunion, Rwanda, St. Helena, Sao Tome and Principe, Senegal, Seychelles, Sierra Leone, Somalia, South Africa, South Sudan, Sudan, Swaziland, Tanzania, Togo, Tunisia, Uganda, Western Sahara, Zambia, Zimbabwe.

ADJUSTMENTS FOR SEASONAL AND TRADING-DAY VARIATIONS

Goods are initially classified under the Harmonized Commodity Description and Coding System (Harmonized System), which is an internationally accepted standard for the commodity classification of traded goods. The Harmonized System describes and measures the characteristics of the goods and is the basis for the systems used in the United States: Schedule B for exports and Harmonized Tariff Schedule for imports. Combining trade into approximately 140 export and 140 import end-use categories makes it possible to examine goods according to their principal uses (see Exhibits 7 and 8). These categories are used as the basis for computing the seasonal and trading-day adjusted data. These adjusted data are then summed to the six end-use aggregates for publication (see Exhibit 6). These data are provided to BEA, from the U.S. Census Bureau, for use in the NIPAs and in the U.S International Transactions Accounts (balance of payments accounts).

Exhibit 19 shows goods (Census Basis) that are seasonally adjusted for selected countries and world areas. Unlike the commodity-based adjustments discussed above, these adjustments are developed and applied directly at the country and world area levels. For total exports and imports, data users should refer to the commodity-based totals shown in the other exhibits. The seasonally adjusted country and world area data will not sum to the seasonally adjusted commodity-based totals because the seasonally adjusted country and world area data and the commodity-based totals are derived from different aggregations of the export and import data and from different seasonal adjustment models. Data users should use caution drawing comparisons between the two sets of seasonally adjusted series.

The seasonal adjustment procedure (X13-ARIMA-SEATS) is based on a model that estimates the monthly movements as percentages above or below the general level of series (unlike other methods that redistribute the actual series values over the calendar year). Because the data series for aircraft is highly variable, users studying data trends may wish to analyze trade in aircraft separately from other trade.

ADJUSTMENTS FOR PRICE CHANGE

Data adjusted for seasonal variation on a real chained-dollar basis (2009 base year) are presented in Exhibits 10 and 11. This adjustment for price change is done using the Fisher chain-weighted methodology. The deflators are primarily based on the monthly price indexes published by the Bureau of Labor Statistics using techniques developed for the NIPAs by BEA.

PRINCIPAL COMMODITIES

Goods data appearing in Exhibit 15 are classified in terms of the SITC Revision 4, with the exception of agricultural and manufactured goods. Agricultural goods are defined by the U.S. Department of Agriculture (USDA); they consist of non-marine food products and other products of agriculture that have not passed through complex processes of manufacture. Manufactured goods conform to the NAICS; they consist of goods that have been mechanically, physically, or chemically transformed. USDA agricultural goods and NAICS manufactured goods are not mutually exclusive categories.

Re-exports are foreign merchandise entering the country as imports and then exported in substantially the same condition as when imported. Re-exports, included in overall export totals, appear as separate line items in Exhibit 15.

ADVANCED TECHNOLOGY PRODUCTS

About 500 of some 22,000 Schedule B and Harmonized Tariff Schedule classification codes used in reporting U.S. merchandise trade are identified as "advanced technology" codes, and they meet the following criteria:

1. The code contains products whose technology is from a recognized high technology field (e.g., biotechnology).
2. These products represent leading edge technology in that field.
3. Such products constitute a significant part of all items covered in the selected classification code.

The aggregation of the goods results in a measure of advanced technology trade that appears in Exhibits 16 and 16a. This product- and commodity-based measure of advanced technology differs from broader NAICS-based measures, which include all goods produced by a particular industry group, regardless of the level of technology embodied in the goods.

GOODS (BALANCE OF PAYMENTS BASIS) AND SERVICES

Quarterly and annual statistics for goods on a balance of payments (BOP) basis and for services are included in the U.S. International Transactions Accounts (ITAs), which are published by BEA in news releases in March, June, September, and December and in the *Survey of Current Business* in the January, April, July, and October issues. The next release of the ITAs is scheduled for March 17, 2016. The *Survey of Current Business* is available online at www.bea.gov/scb/index htm.

GOODS (BALANCE OF PAYMENTS BASIS)

Goods on a Census basis are adjusted by BEA to a BOP basis to align the data with the concepts and definitions used to prepare the international and national economic accounts. These adjustments, which are applied separately to exports and imports, are necessary to supplement coverage of the Census data, to eliminate duplication of transactions recorded elsewhere in the international accounts, and to value transactions at market prices. They include both *additions* to and *deductions* from goods on a Census basis and are presented in this release as *net adjustments*. Adjustments that exhibit significant seasonal patterns are seasonally adjusted. BEA also publishes more detailed quarterly and annual statistics for *net adjustments* in ITA Table 2.4. U.S. International Trade in Goods, Balance of Payments Adjustments and in the January, April, July, and October issues of the *Survey of Current Business*.

The export adjustments include:

Exports under U.S. military sales contracts - This adjustment reflects the net amount of two separate adjustments. BEA first *deducts* goods identified in the Census data as exports under the U.S. Foreign Military Sales program. BEA then *adds* primary source data for these exports, which are reported to BEA by the U.S. Department of Defense.

Gold exports, nonmonetary - This *addition* is made for gold that is purchased by foreign official agencies from private dealers in the United States and held at the Federal Reserve Bank of New York. The Census data only include gold that leaves the U.S. customs territory.

Goods procured in U.S. ports by foreign carriers - This *addition* is made for foreign air and ocean carriers' fuel purchases in U.S. ports.

Net exports of goods under merchanting - This *addition* is made to include the net value of the purchase and subsequent resale of goods abroad without the goods entering the United States. Because these goods do not cross the U.S. customs frontier, their value is not recorded in the Census data.

Other adjustments to exports include:

Deductions for equipment repairs (parts and labor), developed motion picture film, and military grant-aid. *Additions* for sales of fish caught in U.S. territorial waters, exports of electricity to Mexico, private gift parcels, vessels and oil rigs for which ownership changes, valuation of software exports at market value, and low-value (below reporting threshold) transactions for 1999–2009 to phase in a revised Census Bureau low-value methodology that was implemented for goods on a Census basis beginning with statistics for 2010.

The import adjustments include:

Gold imports, nonmonetary - This *addition* is made for gold sold by foreign official agencies to private purchasers out of stock held at the Federal Reserve Bank of New York. The Census data only include gold that enters the U.S. customs territory.

Goods procured in foreign ports by U.S. carriers - This *addition* is made for U.S. air and ocean carriers' fuel purchases in foreign ports.

Imports by U.S. military agencies - This *addition* is made for purchases of goods abroad by U.S. military agencies, which are reported to BEA by the U.S. Department of Defense. The Census data only include imports of goods by U.S. military agencies that enter the U.S. customs territory.

Inland freight in Canada and Mexico - This *addition* is made for inland freight in Canada and Mexico. Imports of goods from all countries should be valued at the customs value—the value at the foreign port of export including inland freight charges. For imports from Canada and Mexico, this should be the cost of the goods at the U.S. border. However, the customs value for imports for certain Canadian and Mexican goods is the point of origin in Canada or Mexico. BEA makes an *addition* for the inland freight charges of transporting these goods to the U.S. border to make the value comparable to the customs value reported for imports from other countries.

Other adjustments to imports include:

Deductions for equipment repairs (parts and labor), repairs to U.S. vessels abroad, and developed motion picture film. *Additions* for non-reported imports of locomotives and railcars, imports of electricity from Mexico, conversion of vessels for commercial use, valuation of software imports at market value, and low-value (below reporting threshold) transactions for 1999–2009 to phase in a revised Census Bureau low-value methodology that was implemented for goods on a Census basis beginning with statistics for 2010.

SERVICES

The services statistics cover transactions between foreign countries and the 50 states, the District of Columbia, Puerto Rico, the U.S. Virgin Islands, and other U.S. territories and possessions. Transactions with U.S. military, diplomatic, and consular installations abroad are excluded because these installations are considered to be part of the U.S. economy.

Services statistics are based on quarterly, annual, and benchmark surveys and information obtained from monthly government and industry reports. For categories for which monthly data are not available, monthly statistics are derived from quarterly statistics through temporal distribution, or interpolation. The interpolation methodology used by BEA is the modified Denton proportional first difference method. This method preserves the pattern of the monthly indicator series, if available, while satisfying the annual aggregation constraints. See "An Empirical Review of Methods for Temporal Distribution and Interpolation in the National Accounts" for more information. Services are seasonally adjusted when statistically significant seasonal patterns are present.

Services are shown in nine broad categories. The following is a brief description of the types of services included in each category:

Maintenance and repair services n i.e. (not included elsewhere) - Consists of maintenance and repair services performed by residents of one country on goods that are owned by residents of another country. The repairs may be performed at the site of the repair facility or elsewhere. Excludes such services in which the cost is included in the price of the goods and is not billed separately or is declared as a part of the price of the goods on the import or export declaration filed with the U.S. Customs and Border Protection. Maintenance and repair of computers are included under computer services, and some maintenance and repair of ships, aircraft, and other transport equipment are included under transport services.

Transport - Consists of transactions associated with moving people and freight from one location to another and includes related supporting and auxiliary services. Transport covers all modes of transportation, including air, sea, rail, road, space, and pipeline. Postal and courier services and port services, which cover cargo handling, storage and warehousing, and other related transport services, are also included.

Travel (for all purposes including education) - Includes goods and services acquired by nonresidents while abroad. A traveler is defined as a person who stays, or intends to stay, for less than one year in a country of which he or she is not a resident or as a nonresident whose purpose is to obtain education or medical treatment, no matter how long the stay. Purchases can be either for own use or for gifts to others. Travel is a transactor-based component that covers a variety of goods and services, primarily lodging, meals, transportation in the country of travel, amusement, entertainment, and gifts. Excludes air passenger services for travel between countries, which are included in *transport*, and goods for resale, which are included in goods.

Travel includes business and personal travel. Business travel covers goods and services acquired for use by persons whose primary purpose for travel is for business (including goods and services for which business travelers are reimbursed by employers). Business travel also includes expenditures by border, seasonal, and other short-term workers in their economy of employment. Personal travel covers travel for all non-business purposes, including for medical or educational purposes.

Insurance services - Includes the direct insurance services of providing life insurance and annuities, non-life (property and casualty) insurance, reinsurance, freight insurance, and auxiliary insurance services. Insurance is measured as gross premiums earned plus premium supplements less claims payable, with an adjustment for claims volatility. Premium supplements represent investment income from insurance reserves, which are attributed to policyholders who are treated as paying the income back to the insurer. Auxiliary insurance services include agents' commissions, brokerage services, insurance consulting services, actuarial services, and other insurance services.

Financial services - Includes financial intermediary and auxiliary services, except insurance services. These services include those normally provided by banks and other financial institutions. Services primarily include those for which an explicit commission or a fee is charged; implicit fees for bond transactions, measured as the difference between bid and ask prices, are also included. Services include securities brokerage and underwriting, financial management, financial advisory, and custody services; credit and other credit-related services; and securities lending, electronic funds transfer, and other services.

Charges for the use of intellectual property n i.e. - Includes charges for the use of proprietary rights, such as patents, trademarks, and copyrights, and charges for licenses to use, reproduce, distribute, and sell or purchase intellectual property.

Telecommunications, computer, and information services - Telecommunications services include the broadcast or transmission of sound, images, data, or other information by electronic means. These services do not include the value of the information transmitted. Computer services consist of hardware- and software-related services and data processing services. Sales of customized software and related use licenses, as well as licenses to use non-customized software with a periodic license fee, are also included, as is software downloaded or otherwise electronically delivered. Cross-border transactions in non-customized packaged software with a license for perpetual use are included in goods. Information services include news agency services, database services, and web search portals.

Other business services - Consists of research and development services, professional and management consulting services, and technical, trade-related, and other business services. Research and development services include services associated with basic and applied research and experimental development of new products and processes. Professional and management consulting services include legal services, accounting, management consulting, managerial services, public relations services, advertising, and market research. Amounts received by a parent company from its affiliates for general overhead expenses related to these services are included. Technical, trade-related, and other business services include architectural and engineering, construction, audio-visual, waste treatment, operational leasing, trade-related, and other business services.

Government goods and services n.i.e. - Includes goods and services supplied by and to enclaves, such as embassies, military bases, and international organizations; goods and services acquired from the host economy by diplomats, consular staff, and military personnel located abroad and their dependents; and services supplied by and to governments that are not included in other services categories. Services supplied by and to governments are classified to specific services categories when source data permit.

GOODS (BOP BASIS) AND SERVICES BY COUNTRY AND AREA

Monthly country and area detail is not available for goods on a BOP basis or for services. However, quarterly statistics on goods on a BOP basis and on services that are seasonally adjusted by geography are shown in Exhibit 20. Unlike the seasonal adjustments by commodity and by service type that are applied to the global totals, these adjustments are developed and applied directly at the country and world area levels. For total exports and imports, data users should refer to the by-commodity and by-service type totals shown in the other exhibits. The seasonally adjusted country and world area data will not sum to the seasonally adjusted by-commodity and by-service type totals because the two sets of statistics are derived from different aggregations of the export and import data and from different seasonal adjustment models. Data users should use caution drawing comparisons between the two sets of seasonally adjusted series.

The definitions of the world areas shown in Exhibit 20 are consistent with the definitions for goods on a Census basis (see *AREA GROUPINGS* above) with a few exceptions. For services, CAFTA-DR is not available because trade with this area's member countries cannot be separately identified. For goods on a BOP basis and for services, European Union and OPEC reflect the composition of the areas as they were at the time of reporting.

REVISION PROCEDURE (GOODS ON A BOP BASIS AND SERVICES)

Monthly Revisions: Each month, a preliminary estimate for the current month and a revised estimate for the immediately preceding month are released. After the initial revision, no further revisions are made to a month until more complete source data become available in March, June, September, and December.

Quarterly Revisions: The releases in March, June, September, and December contain revised estimates for the previous six months to incorporate more comprehensive and updated source data.

Annual Revisions: Each June, historical data are revised to incorporate newly available and revised source data, changes in definitions and classifications, and changes in estimation methods. Seasonally adjusted data are also revised to reflect recalculated seasonal and trading-day adjustments.

Other Revisions: The release in February contains revisions to goods for January through November of the most recent year and the release in March contains revisions to both goods and services for all months of the most recent year. These revisions result from forcing the seasonally adjusted months to equal the annual totals.

DATA AVAILABILITY

The U.S. International Trade in Goods and Services news release (FT-900) and the FT-900 Supplement are available at the following:

www.census.gov/ft900

www.bea.gov/newsreleases/international/trade/tradnewsrelease.htm

MONTHLY RELEASE SCHEDULE

Statistical Month	Date	Day
January	03-04-16	Friday
February	04-05-16	Tuesday
March	05-04-16	Wednesday
April	06-03-16	Friday
May	07-06-16	Wednesday
June	08-05-16	Friday
July	09-02-16	Friday
August	10-05-16	Wednesday
September	11-04-16	Friday
October	12-06-16	Tuesday

U.S. Census Bureau News

U.S. Department of Commerce • Washington, D.C. 20230

FOR IMMEDIATE RELEASE
8:30 A.M. EST FRIDAY, MARCH 4, 2016

For information on goods contact:
U.S. Census Bureau:
Matthew Przybocki (301) 763-2311

FT-900 SUPPLEMENT
January 2016

FT-900 Supplement

Exhibit 1. Exports, Imports, and Balance of Goods by Selected NAICS-Based Product Code, Not Seasonally Adjusted: January 2016

In millions of dollars. Details may not equal total due to rounding. (X) Not Applicable. (-) Represents zero or less than one-half unit of measurement shown.

NAICS-Based Product Code Description	Balance		Exports		Imports for Consumption (Customs Value)			
					Totals		Calculated Duty	
	January	Year-to-Date	January	Year-to-Date	January	Year-to-Date	January	Year-to-Date
GRAND TOTAL	**-56,600.9**	**-56,600.9**	**108,453.3**	**108,453.3**	**165,054.1**	**165,054.1**	**2,691.2**	**2,691.2**
Agricultural, Forestry & Fishery Products	243.1	243.1	5,461.9	5,461.9	5,218.8	5,218.8	5.9	5.9
(Domestic)								
Agricultural Products, Total	1,535.7	1,535.7	4,934.2	4,934.2	3,398.5	3,398.5	4.8	4.8
Livestock And Livestock Products	-292.5	-292.5	144.4	144.4	436.9	436.9	0.4	0.4
Forestry Products	-9.8	-9.8	165.8	165.8	175.5	175.5	0.2	0.2
Fish, Fresh Or Chilled; And Other Marine Products	-990.3	-990.3	217.5	217.5	1,207.8	1,207.8	0.5	0.5
Mining, Total	-4,710.4	-4,710.4	2,119.9	2,119.9	6,830.3	6,830.3	6.8	6.8
(Domestic)								
Oil And Gas	-5,124.7	-5,124.7	1,307.3	1,307.3	6,432.0	6,432.0	6.6	6.6
Minerals And Ores	414.4	414.4	812.6	812.6	398.2	398.2	0.2	0.2
Manufacturing, Total	-66,048.5	-66,048.5	79,230.3	79,230.3	145,278.8	145,278.8	2,663.8	2,663.8
(Domestic)								
Food And Kindred Products	-228.8	-228.8	4,453.8	4,453.8	4,682.6	4,682.6	77.4	77.4
Beverages And Tobacco	-1,030.7	-1,030.7	481.3	481.3	1,512.0	1,512.0	6.5	6.5
Textile And Fabrics	0.5	0.5	668.5	668.5	667.9	667.9	31.1	31.1
Textile Mill Products	-1,427.8	-1,427.8	206.4	206.4	1,634.1	1,634.1	103.0	103.0
Apparel And Accessories	-6,796.5	-6,796.5	223.8	223.8	7,020.3	7,020 3	983.5	983.5
Leather And Allied Products	-3,201.5	-3,201.5	218.3	218.3	3,419.7	3,419.7	357.9	357.9
Wood Products	-837.7	-837.7	525.0	525.0	1,362.7	1,362.7	16.2	16.2
Paper Products	301.3	301.3	1,844.6	1,844.6	1,543.3	1,543.3	3.4	3.4
Printing, Publishing & Similar Products	-44.1	-44.1	354.8	354.8	398.9	398.9	0.2	0.2
Petroleum And Coal Products	1,210.4	1,210.4	5,119.7	5,119.7	3,909.3	3,909.3	9.5	9.5
Chemicals	-1,828.0	-1,828.0	14,167.3	14,167.3	15,995.3	15,995.3	127.0	127.0
Plastic And Rubber Products (1)	-1,690.4	-1,690.4	2,201.1	2,201.1	3,891.4	3,891.4	96.9	96.9
Nonmetallic Mineral Products (1)	-845.0	-845.0	834.6	834.6	1,679.6	1,679.6	56.1	56.1
Primary Metal Products	-2,373.4	-2,373.4	3,435.2	3,435.2	5,808.5	5,808.5	21.5	21.5
Fabricated Metal Products	-2,039.9	-2,039.9	3,091.6	3,091.6	5,131.5	5,131.5	109.5	109.5
Machinery, Except Electrical	-3,041.9	-3,041.9	8,587.3	8,587.3	11,629.1	11,629.1	89.2	89.2
Computers and Electronic Products (1)	-18,372.7	-18,372.7	8,872.8	8,872.8	27,245.5	27,245 5	70.5	70.5
Electrical Equipment, Appliances and Components (1)	-4,293.1	-4,293.1	3,472.5	3,472.5	7,765.6	7,765.6	142.3	142.3
Transportation Equipment (1)	-11,423.8	-11,423.8	16,715.2	16,715.2	28,139.0	28,139.0	258.2	258.2
Furniture and Fixtures	-2,899.8	-2,899.8	370.1	370.1	3,269.9	3,269.9	5.9	5.9
Miscellaneous Manufactured Commodities	-5,185.7	-5,185.7	3,386.7	3,386.7	8,572.3	8,572.3	98.1	98.1
Special Classification Provisions	-2,673.5	-2,673.5	5,052.7	5,052.7	7,726.3	7,726.3	14.8	14.8
(Domestic)								
Scrap & Waste	847.5	847.5	1,161.6	1,161.6	314.1	314.1	(-)	(-)
Used Or Second-Hand Merchandise (1)	-23.1	-23.1	810.5	810.5	833.5	833.5	1.3	1.3
Goods Returned Or Reimported	-4,886.3	-4,886.3	0.8	0.8	4,887.1	4,887.1	0.2	0.2
Special Classification Provision, Nspf	1,388.3	1,388.3	3,079.8	3,079.8	1,691.5	1,691.5	13.3	13.3
Re-exports	16,588.4	16,588.4	16,588.4	16 588.4	(X)	(X)	(X)	(X)
Timing Adjustments	(X)	(X)	(X)	(X)	(X)	(X)	(X)	(X)

(1) Export statis ics for certain commodity classifications related to the aircraft industry are subject to suppression and have been aggregated in a manner that prevents the disclosure of confiden ial informa ion. For additional information, see www.census.gov/foreign-trade/statistics/no ices/aircraft/.

Exhibit 2. Origin of Movement of U. S. Exports of Goods by State by NAICS-Based Product Code Groupings, Not Seasonally Adjusted: 2016

In millions of dollars. Foreign Trade Zone (FTZ) shipments are included in the U. S. total and distributed among individual states and territories. Separate FTZ total line is for reference only. Details may not equal totals due to rounding. (X) Not applicable. (-) Represents zero or less than one-half unit of measurement shown.

Item	NAICS-Based Product Code Groupings						Re-exports		Total	
	Manufactured Commodities			Non-Manufactured Commodities (1)						
	January	Year-to-Date		January	Year-to-Date		January	Year-to-Date	January	Year-to-Date
		Total	Percent		Total	Percent				
U.S. Total	**79,230.3**	**79,230.3**	**100.0**	**10,737.2**	**10,737.2**	**100.0**	**16,588.4**	**16,588.4**	**108,453.3**	**108,453.3**
Foreign Trade Zone	1,911.5	1,911.5	2.4	(-)	(-)	(-)	184.5	184.5	2,096.0	2,096.0
Alabama	1,439.6	1,439.6	1 8	71.5	71.5	0.7	71.7	71.7	1,582.8	1,582.8
Alaska	45.9	45.9	0.1	58.6	58.6	0.5	2.0	2.0	106.5	106.5
Arizona	985.9	985.9	1 2	277.2	277.2	2.6	455.2	455.2	1,718.3	1,718.3
Arkansas	322.1	322.1	0.4	55.5	55.5	0.5	19.4	19.4	397.0	397.0
California	7,825.8	7,825.8	9 9	1,276.4	1,276.4	11.9	2,861.1	2,861.1	11,963.3	11,963.3
Colorado	515.0	515.0	0.7	19.3	19.3	0.2	65.5	65.5	599.8	599.8
Connecticut	994.3	994.3	1.3	34.8	34.8	0.3	81.3	81.3	1,110.5	1,110.5
Delaware	227.3	227.3	0.3	9.3	9.3	0.1	110.5	110.5	347.0	347.0
Florida	2,839.3	2,839.3	3.6	281.6	281.6	2.6	876.0	876.0	3,997.0	3,997.0
Georgia	2,120.5	2,120.5	2.7	212 2	212.2	2.0	276.0	276.0	2,608.7	2,608.7
Hawaii	41.9	41.9	0.1	6.1	6.1	0.1	1.7	1.7	49.8	49 8
Idaho	205.7	205.7	0.3	46.7	46.7	0.4	80.6	80.6	333.1	333.1
Illinois	3,433.1	3,433.1	4 3	375.9	375.9	3.5	873.7	873.7	4,682.7	4,682.7
Indiana	2,360.5	2,360.5	3 0	66.6	66.6	0.6	273.8	273.8	2,700.9	2,700.9
Iowa	740.0	740.0	0 9	117.2	117.2	1.1	30.4	30.4	887.6	887.6
Kansas	466.5	466.5	0.6	118.8	118.8	1.1	53.5	53.5	638.7	638.7
Kentucky	1,670.4	1,670.4	2.1	19.7	19.7	0.2	419.6	419.6	2,109.7	2,109.7
Louisiana	2,156.1	2,156.1	2.7	1,445.3	1,445.3	13.5	33.8	33.8	3,635.1	3,635.1
Maine	118.1	118.1	0.1	63.5	63.5	0.6	11.3	11.3	192.9	192.9
Maryland	514.9	514.9	0.6	50.2	50.2	0.5	113.6	113.6	678.7	678.7
Massachusetts	1,579.3	1,579.3	2.0	247.8	247.8	2.3	297.7	297.7	2,124.8	2,124.8
Michigan	3,337.2	3,337.2	4.2	177.4	177.4	1.7	473.3	473.3	3,987.9	3,987.9
Minnesota	1,217.8	1,217.8	1.5	99.6	99.6	0.9	158.7	158.7	1,476.0	1,476.0
Mississippi	716.8	716.8	0.9	23.4	23.4	0.2	103.6	103.6	843.7	843.7
Missouri	724.9	724.9	0.9	63.5	63.5	0.6	67.3	67.3	855.7	855.7
Montana	70.4	70.4	0.1	16.4	16.4	0.2	15.5	15.5	102.4	102.4
Nebraska	383.8	383.8	0 5	45.8	45.8	0.4	20.1	20.1	449.7	449.7
Nevada	483.7	483.7	0.6	29.0	29.0	0.3	105.4	105.4	618.2	618.2
New Hampshire	337.1	337.1	0.4	15.0	15.0	0.1	58.9	58.9	411.0	411.0
New Jersey	1,630.7	1,630.7	2.1	177.2	177.2	1.7	470.3	470.3	2,278.2	2,278.2
New Mexico	124.1	124.1	0.2	13.5	13.5	0.1	121.9	121.9	259.5	259.5
New York	2,666.3	2,666.3	3.4	690.4	690.4	6.4	1,842.6	1,842.6	5,199.3	5,199.3
North Carolina	1,859.0	1,859.0	2.3	156.3	156.3	1.5	203.4	203.4	2,218.8	2,218.8
North Dakota	140.7	140.7	0.2	176.6	176.6	1.6	5.3	5.3	322.5	322.5
Ohio	3,068.6	3,068.6	3.9	217.1	217.1	2.0	404.2	404.2	3,689.9	3,689.9
Oklahoma	312.6	312.6	0.4	15.6	15.6	0.1	39.6	39.6	367.7	367.7
Oregon	1,162.7	1,162.7	1.5	191.1	191.1	1.8	133.7	133.7	1,487.5	1,487.5
Pennsylvania	2,254.4	2,254.4	2 8	182.6	182.6	1.7	448.8	448.8	2,885.8	2,885.8
Rhode Island	111.2	111.2	0.1	34.6	34.6	0.3	15.0	15.0	160.8	160.8
Sou h Carolina	1,529.7	1,529.7	1 9	37.0	37.0	0.3	122.2	122.2	1,688.9	1,688.9
Sou h Dakota	93.7	93.7	0.1	5.6	5.6	0.1	2.3	2.3	101.6	101.6
Tennessee	1,764.9	1,764.9	2 2	79.9	79.9	0.7	565.4	565.4	2,410.3	2,410.3
Texas	13,566.1	13,566.1	17.1	1,439.1	1,439.1	13.4	3,578.5	3,578.5	18,583.7	18,583.7
Utah	600.0	600.0	0.8	16.8	16.8	0.2	31.6	31.6	648.5	648.5
Vermont	163.8	163.8	0.2	5.1	5.1	(-)	69.5	69.5	238.3	238.3
Virginia	931.0	931.0	1.2	247 3	247.3	2.3	137.1	137.1	1,315.4	1,315.4
Washington	4,249.2	4,249.2	5.4	1,045.1	1,045.1	9.7	202.8	202.8	5,497.1	5,497.1
West Virginia	285.5	285.5	0.4	103.1	103.1	1.0	7.8	7.8	396.5	396.5
Wisconsin	1,351.4	1,351.4	1.7	112.1	112.1	1.0	126.2	126.2	1,589.7	1,589.7
Wyoming	71.4	71.4	0.1	3.1	3.1	(-)	0.3	0.3	74.8	74.8
Dist of Columbia	33.1	33.1	(-)	4.3	4.3	(-)	0.7	0.7	38.1	38.1
Puerto Rico	1,958.4	1,958.4	2 5	6.2	6.2	0.1	46.5	46.5	2,011.2	2,011.2
US Virgin Islands	2.0	2.0	(-)	0.2	0.2	(-)	1.1	1.1	3.2	3.2
Other	1,425.9	1,425.9	1 8	452.8	452.8	4.2	0.6	0.6	3,776.7	3,776.7
Estimated Shipments	(X)	(X)	(X)	(X)	(X)	(X)	(X)	(X)	1,897.4	1,897.4
Unreported (2)	1,425.9	1,425.9	1.8	452.8	452.8	4.2	0.6	0.6	1,879.3	1,879.3
Timing Adjustment	(X)	(X)	(X)	(X)	(X)	(X)	(X)	(X)	(X)	(-)

(1) Includes agricultural, forestry, fishery products, mineral commodities, scrap, waste and used or second-hand merchandise. The state of origin of movement value totals for non-manufactured commodities usually reflect the state where the U.S. port of export is located.

(2) Includes prior month's revision to exports to Canada.

Exhibit 2a. U. S. General Imports of Goods by State, State of Destination, by NAICS-Based Product Code Groupings, Not Seasonally Adjusted: 2016

In millions of dollars. Foreign Trade Zone (FTZ) shipments are included in the U. S. total and distributed among individual states and territories. Separate FTZ total line is for reference only. Details may not equal totals due to rounding. (X) Not applicable.
(-) Represents zero or less than one-half unit of measurement shown.

Item	NAICS-Based Product Code Groupings						Total		
	Manufactured Commodities			Non-Manufactured Commodities (1)					
	January	Year-to-Date		January	Year-to-Date		January	Year-to-Date	
		Total	Percent		Total	Percent		Total	Percent
U.S. Total	**144,666.0**	**144,666.0**	**100.0**	**19,893.9**	**19,893.9**	**100.0**	**165,847.8**	**165,847.8**	**100.0**
Foreign Trade Zone	12,854.2	12,854.2	8.9	4,064.1	4,064.1	20.4	16,918.2	16,918.2	10.2
Alabama	1,568.1	1,568.1	1.1	155.9	155.9	0.8	1,724.0	1,724.0	1.0
Alaska	89.0	89.0	0.1	46.6	46.6	0.2	135.5	135.5	0.1
Arizona	1,183.6	1,183.6	0.8	563.6	563.6	2.8	1,747.2	1,747.2	1.1
Arkansas	601.2	601.2	0.4	13.0	13.0	0.1	614.2	614.2	0.4
California	28,140.4	28,140.4	19.5	3,006.5	3,006.5	15.1	31,146.9	31,146.9	18.8
Colorado	804.9	804.9	0.6	149.6	149.6	0.8	954.5	954.5	0.6
Connecticut	1,163.0	1,163.0	0.8	172.9	172.9	0.9	1,335.9	1,335.9	0.8
Delaware	295.0	295.0	0.2	241.7	241.7	1.2	536.7	536.7	0.3
Florida	4,645.6	4,645.6	3.2	1,169.4	1,169.4	5.9	5,815.0	5,815.0	3.5
Georgia	6,157.7	6,157.7	4.3	169.3	169.3	0.9	6,327.0	6,327.0	3.8
Hawaii	89.8	89.8	0.1	120.8	120.8	0.6	210.5	210.5	0.1
Idaho	292.0	292.0	0.2	26.7	26.7	0.1	318.7	318.7	0.2
Illinois	6,851.5	6,851.5	4.7	1,496.3	1,496.3	7.5	8,347.9	8,347.9	5.0
Indiana	3,463.1	3,463.1	2.4	217.9	217.9	1.1	3,681.0	3,681.0	2.2
Iowa	579.8	579.8	0.4	94.4	94.4	0.5	674.2	674.2	0.4
Kansas	852.5	852.5	0.6	95.1	95.1	0.5	947.6	947.6	0.6
Kentucky	2,695.9	2,695.9	1.9	181.1	181.1	0.9	2,876.9	2,876.9	1.7
Louisiana	1,163.5	1,163.5	0.8	1,068.4	1,068.4	5.4	2,231.9	2,231.9	1.3
Maine	230.0	230.0	0.2	81.3	81.3	0.4	311.3	311.3	0.2
Maryland	2,332.6	2,332.6	1.6	131.6	131.6	0.7	2,464.2	2,464.2	1.5
Massachusetts	2,164.4	2,164.4	1.5	399.7	399.7	2.0	2,564.1	2,564.1	1.5
Michigan	9,206.1	9,206.1	6.4	702.3	702.3	3.5	9,908.4	9,908.4	6.0
Minnesota	1,568.1	1,568.1	1.1	424.4	424.4	2.1	1,992.5	1,992.5	1.2
Mississippi	828.4	828.4	0.6	140.4	140.4	0.7	968.8	968.8	0.6
Missouri	1,361.8	1,361.8	0.9	149.0	149.0	0.7	1,510.9	1,510.9	0.9
Montana	59.1	59.1	(-)	193.3	193.3	1.0	252.4	252.4	0.2
Nebraska	285.4	285.4	0.2	24.3	24.3	0.1	309.8	309.8	0.2
Nevada	752.2	752.2	0.5	27.0	27.0	0.1	779.1	779.1	0.5
New Hampshire	620.6	620.6	0.4	29.0	29.0	0.1	649.6	649.6	0.4
New Jersey	7,481.5	7,481.5	5.2	900.9	900.9	4.5	8,382.4	8,382.4	5.1
New Mexico	157.2	157.2	0.1	47.0	47.0	0.2	204.2	204.2	0.1
New York	8,211.4	8,211.4	5.7	1,565.9	1,565.9	7.9	9,777.3	9,777.3	5.9
North Carolina	3,390.9	3,390.9	2.3	169.4	169.4	0.9	3,560.3	3,560.3	2.1
North Dakota	141.1	141.1	0.1	54.5	54.5	0.3	195.6	195.6	0.1
Ohio	4,534.3	4,534.3	3.1	337.2	337.2	1.7	4,871.5	4,871.5	2.9
Oklahoma	542.3	542.3	0.4	330.9	330.9	1.7	873.1	873.1	0.5
Oregon	1,302.7	1,302.7	0.9	128.5	128.5	0.6	1,431.2	1,431.2	0.9
Pennsylvania	5,302.3	5,302.3	3.7	638.7	638.7	3.2	5,941.0	5,941.0	3.6
Rhode Island	421.1	421.1	0.3	18.6	18.6	0.1	439.7	439.7	0.3
South Carolina	2,909.0	2,909.0	2.0	87.2	87.2	0.4	2,996.2	2,996.2	1.8
South Dakota	63.7	63.7	(-)	7.4	7.4	(-)	71.1	71.1	(-)
Tennessee	5,570.3	5,570.3	3.9	168.3	168.3	0.8	5,738.6	5,738.6	3.5
Texas	15,045.0	15,045.0	10.4	2,710.8	2,710.8	13.6	17,755.8	17,755.8	10.7
Utah	848.5	848.5	0.6	83.8	83.8	0.4	932.4	932.4	0.6
Vermont	215.1	215.1	0.1	108.9	108.9	0.5	324.1	324.1	0.2
Virginia	1,749.4	1,749.4	1.2	159.8	159.8	0.8	1,909.2	1,909.2	1.2
Washington	3,180.8	3,180.8	2.2	819.3	819.3	4.1	4,000.1	4,000.1	2.4
West Virginia	269.2	269.2	0.2	9.5	9.5	(-)	278.7	278.7	0.2
Wisconsin	1,735.0	1,735.0	1.2	98.4	98.4	0.5	1,833.4	1,833.4	1.1
Wyoming	42.1	42.1	(-)	33.9	33.9	0.2	76.0	76.0	(-)
Dist of Columbia	20.6	20.6	(-)	2.8	2.8	(-)	23.3	23.3	(-)
Puerto Rico	1,235.4	1,235.4	0.9	93.4	93.4	0.5	1,328.8	1,328.8	0.8
US Virgin Islands	10.4	10.4	(-)	0.6	0.6	(-)	11.0	11.0	(-)
Other	241.4	241.4	0.2	26.6	26.6	0.1	1,555.9	1,555.9	0.9
Estimated Shipments	(X)	(X)	(X)	(X)	(X)	(X)	1,287.9	1,287.9	0.8
Unreported	241.4	241.4	0.2	26.6	26.6	0.1	268.0	268.0	0.2
Timing Adjustment	(X)	(X)	(X)	(X)	(X)	(X)	(X)	(X)	(X)

(1) Includes agricultural, forestry, fishery products, mineral commodities, scrap, waste and used or second-hand merchandise.

Exhibit 3. Exports, Imports, and Trade Balance of Goods

In millions of dollars. Details may not equal totals due to seasonal adjustment and rounding.(R) - Revised.

Period	Balance		Exports	Imports	
	Customs	C.I.F.	F.A.S. Value	Customs value	C.I.F. Value
			Seasonally Adjusted		
2015					
Jan.- Dec. (R)	-736,018.6	-803,031.7	1,504,913.9	2,240,932.5	2,307,945.6
Jan. - (R)	-61,098.0	-66,682.3	128,461.3	189,559.4	195,143.6
January (R)	-61,098.0	-66,682.3	128,461.3	189,559.4	195,143.6
February (R)	-55,968.0	-61,557.2	125,589.1	181,557.1	187,146.3
March (R)	-69,289.7	-75,560.4	126,114.0	195,403.6	201,674.4
April (R)	-59,434.5	-65,116.4	128,440.4	187,874.9	193,556.8
May (R)	-59,608.6	-65,180.2	127,056.2	186,664.9	192,236.5
June (R)	-62,349.9	-67,765.8	126,592.4	188,942.4	194,358.2
July (R)	-59,300.2	-64,823.8	127,794.7	187,094.9	192,618.5
August (R)	-66,273.4	-71,879.1	123,760.1	190,033.6	195,639.3
September (R)	-59,464.8	-65,085.9	126,411.9	185,876.7	191,497.7
October (R)	-61,846.4	-67,183.6	123,261.2	185,107.6	190,444.8
November (R)	-60,033.6	-65,370.2	121,169.4	181,203.0	186,539.6
December (R)	-61,351.4	-66,826.8	120,263.2	181,614.6	187,090.0
2016					
Jan.-	-62,397.7	-67,728.6	116,386.5	178,784.3	184,115.1
January	-62,397.7	-67,728.6	116,386.5	178,784.3	184,115.1
February					
March					
April					
May					
June					
July					
August					
September					
October					
November					
December					
			Not Seasonally Adjusted		
2015					
Jan.- Dec.	-736,018.6	-803,031.7	1,504,913.9	2,240,932.5	2,307,945.6
Jan.-	-58,715.5	-64,173.4	121,397.9	180,113.5	185,571.3
January	-58,715.5	-64,173.4	121,397.9	180,113.5	185,571.3
February	-43,898.8	-48,968.5	118,347.5	162,246.3	167,316.0
March	-63,101.6	-69,374.5	133,784.6	196,886.2	203,159.1
April	-60,367.2	-66,130.7	128,505.0	188,872.2	194,635.7
May	-56,931.9	-62,523.6	128,259.5	185,191.4	190,783.1
June	-64,939.2	-70,560.2	130,994.3	195,933.5	201,554.5
July	-68,527.2	-74,292.0	124,391.2	192,918.4	198,683.2
August	-67,083.8	-72,742.8	123,011.1	190,094.9	195,753.9
September	-66,165.6	-71,898.3	125,281.3	191,446.9	197,179.7
October	-65,036.4	-70,581.3	130,462.6	195,498.9	201,043.9
November	-61,486.3	-66,701.4	120,570.2	182,056.5	187,271.6
December (R)	-59,765.2	-65,085.0	119,908.7	179,673.9	184,993.7
2016					
Jan.-	-57,394.5	-62,493.0	108,453.3	165,847.8	170,946.3
January	-57,394.5	-62,493.0	108,453.3	165,847.8	170,946.3
February					
March					
April					
May					
June					
July					
August					
September					
October					
November					
December					

Exhibit 4. Exports, Imports, and Trade Balance of Goods by Country and Area, Not Seasonally Adjusted: 2016

In millions of dollars. Details may not equal totals due to rounding. (X) Not applicable. (-) Represents zero or less than one-half unit of measurement shown.

Country	Balance (Customs imports)			Exports Domestic & Foreign, F.A.S. basis			Imports Customs basis			Imports C.I.F. basis		
	January	Year-to-Date	Rank	January	Year-to-Date	Rank	January	Year-to-Date	Rank	January	Year-to-Date	Rank
TOTAL	**-57,394.5**	**-57,394.5**	**(X)**	**108,453.3**	**108,453.3**	**(X)**	**165,847.8**	**165,847.8**	**(X)**	**170,946.3**	**170,946.3**	**(X)**
Afghanistan	171.9	171.9	218	173.8	173.8	54	1.8	1.8	147	1.9	1.9	148
Albania	0.1	0.1	114	1.8	1.8	177	1.6	1.6	150	1.7	1.7	150
Algeria	-57.1	-57.1	45	111.0	111.0	63	168.2	168.2	61	181.4	181.4	61
Andorra	-0.8	-0.8	83	0.7	0.7	195	1.5	1.5	152	1.5	1.5	152
Angola	-21.0	-21.0	56	191.8	191.8	51	212.9	212.9	57	225.7	225.7	57
Anguilla	2.7	2.7	152	3.1	3.1	159	0.4	0.4	180	0.4	0.4	180
Antigua and Barbuda	11.5	11.5	178	15.0	15.0	114	3.4	3.4	134	3.4	3.4	136
Argentina	405.0	405.0	225	678.3	678.3	31	273.3	273.3	51	289.1	289.1	51
Armenia	-1.6	-1.6	79	3.0	3.0	161	4.6	4.6	128	4.8	4.8	128
Aruba	83.2	83.2	209	84.0	84.0	72	0.8	0.8	162	0.8	0.8	163
Australia*	693.0	693.0	228	1,517.9	1,517.9	16	824.9	824.9	27	850.1	850.1	28
Austria	351.3	351.3	223	1,083.1	1,083.1	22	731.7	731.7	29	748.2	748.2	29
Azerbaijan	22.3	22.3	190	22.9	22.9	102	0.6	0.6	170	0.6	0.6	171
Bahamas	124.8	124.8	216	145.5	145.5	57	20.7	20.7	99	21.4	21.4	99
Bahrain*	-3.1	-3.1	73	56.9	56.9	82	60.0	60.0	75	61.9	61.9	76
Bangladesh	-502.5	-502.5	20	45.7	45.7	86	548.2	548.2	37	567.3	567.3	37
Barbados	31.0	31.0	197	33.5	33.5	91	2.5	2.5	139	2.6	2.6	140
Belarus	-0.4	-0.4	89	4.4	4.4	147	4.8	4.8	126	5.2	5.2	125
Belgium	1,302.1	1,302.1	230	2,580.9	2,580.9	10	1,278.8	1,278.8	22	1,314.6	1,314.6	21
Belize	15.4	15.4	182	18.7	18.7	109	3.3	3.3	135	3.5	3.5	135
Benin	27.7	27.7	196	27.9	27.9	96	0.3	0.3	187	0.3	0.3	186
Bermuda	26.2	26.2	194	27.1	27.1	97	0.8	0.8	161	0.9	0.9	160
Bhutan	-0.4	-0.4	90	0.1	0.1	210	0.5	0.5	173	0.6	0.6	173
Bolivia	5.0	5.0	167	62.9	62.9	80	57.9	57.9	77	58.5	58.5	77
Bosnia and Herzegovina	-4.4	-4.4	72	1.0	1.0	189	5.3	5.3	123	5.5	5.5	123
Botswana	-5.8	-5.8	69	4.8	4.8	143	10.6	10.6	112	11.1	11.1	113
Brazil	363.5	363.5	224	2,087.1	2,087.1	13	1,723.6	1,723.6	18	1,806.7	1,806.7	18
British Indian Ocean Territories	-0.3	-0.3	91	(-)	(-)	216	0.3	0.3	185	0.3	0.3	187
British Virgin Islands	14.8	14.8	181	16.7	16.7	111	1.8	1.8	146	1.9	1.9	147
Brunei	8.9	8.9	173	10.0	10.0	127	1.0	1.0	155	1.1	1.1	155
Bulgaria	-32.6	-32.6	51	14.0	14.0	116	46.6	46.6	82	48.3	48.3	82
Burkina Faso	3.9	3.9	159	4.1	4.1	150	0.2	0.2	193	0.2	0.2	193
Burma	0.3	0.3	120	15.1	15.1	113	14.8	14.8	103	15.3	15.3	103
Burundi	1.9	1.9	145	2.9	2.9	162	1.0	1.0	156	1.0	1.0	156
Cabo Verde	0.4	0.4	123	0.8	0.8	192	0.3	0.3	182	0.3	0.3	183
Cambodia	-193.9	-193.9	27	33.3	33.3	93	227.2	227.2	55	235.6	235.6	55
Cameroon	7.8	7.8	171	13.2	13.2	120	5.5	5.5	122	5.8	5.8	122
Canada**	-2,365.4	-2,365.4	8	19,798.9	19,798.9	1	22,164.3	22,164.3	3	22,726.1	22,726.1	2
Cayman Islands	44.9	44.9	200	49.5	49.5	83	4.6	4.6	127	4.6	4.6	129
Central African Republic	0.8	0.8	130	0.9	0.9	190	(-)	(-)	214	(-)	(-)	214
Chad	-57.5	-57.5	44	1.8	1.8	176	59.3	59.3	76	63.3	63.3	75
Chile*	440.4	440.4	226	1,251.0	1,251.0	19	810.6	810.6	28	893.8	893.8	27
China	-28,933.5	-28,933.5	1	8,212.1	8,212.1	3	37,145.7	37,145.7	1	38,728.7	38,728.7	1
Christmas Island	-0.2	-0.2	92	(-)	(-)	223	0.2	0.2	190	0.2	0.2	191
Cocos (Keeling) Islands	-0.7	-0.7	85	0.1	0.1	214	0.7	0.7	164	0.7	0.7	167
Colombia*	116.8	116.8	215	1,021.9	1,021.9	23	905.1	905.1	26	960.6	960.6	26
Comoros	(-)	(-)	100	(-)	(-)	218	(-)	(-)	207	(-)	(-)	206
Congo (Brazzaville)	-2.7	-2.7	75	6.4	6.4	134	9.1	9.1	115	9.7	9.7	115
Congo (Kinshasa)	2.7	2.7	151	4.5	4.5	144	1.8	1.8	148	1.8	1.8	149
Cook Islands	-0.1	-0.1	94	0.2	0.2	203	0.4	0.4	179	0.4	0.4	181
Costa Rica**	150.3	150.3	217	444.0	444.0	38	293.7	293.7	46	311.6	311.6	46
Cote d'Ivoire	-109.6	-109.6	37	18.4	18.4	110	128.0	128.0	66	131.3	131.3	67
Croatia	-16.9	-16.9	59	20.0	20.0	108	36.9	36.9	87	37.9	37.9	87
Cuba	23.1	23.1	191	23.1	23.1	101	(-)	(-)	(X)	(-)	(-)	(X)
Curacao	36.1	36.1	199	45.9	45.9	85	9.8	9.8	113	10.1	10.1	114
Cyprus	1.5	1.5	141	3.5	3.5	156	2.0	2.0	144	2.1	2.1	143
Czech Republic	-130.9	-130.9	32	182.7	182.7	52	313.6	313.6	44	323.0	323.0	45
Denmark	-564.2	-564.2	19	135.1	135.1	59	699.4	699.4	31	711.7	711.7	33
Djibouti	12.8	12.8	179	13.4	13.4	118	0.6	0.6	169	0.6	0.6	170
Dominica	4.4	4.4	162	4.5	4.5	145	0.1	0.1	200	0.1	0.1	200
Dominican Republic**	264.6	264.6	221	508.2	508.2	37	243.6	243.6	52	249.6	249.6	52
Ecuador	-174.4	-174.4	30	379.8	379.8	41	554.2	554.2	36	604.8	604.8	35
Egypt	110.5	110.5	213	237.8	237.8	48	127.2	127.2	67	132.6	132.6	66
El Salvador**	63.6	63.6	205	226.8	226.8	49	163.2	163.2	62	168.4	168.4	62
Equatorial Guinea	-9.7	-9.7	65	2.1	2.1	172	11.8	11.8	110	13.4	13.4	108
Eritrea	0.2	0.2	115	0.2	0.2	206	(-)	(-)	223	(-)	(-)	223

Exhibit 4. Exports, Imports, and Trade Balance of Goods by Country and Area, Not Seasonally Adjusted: 2016

In millions of dollars. Details may not equal totals due to rounding. (X) Not applicable. (-) Represents zero or less than one-half unit of measurement shown.

Country	Balance (Customs imports)			Exports Domestic & Foreign, F.A.S. basis			Imports Customs basis			Imports C.I.F. basis		
	January	Year-to-Date	Rank	January	Year-to-Date	Rank	January	Year-to-Date	Rank	January	Year-to-Date	Rank
Estonia	-31.3	-31.3	52	16.6	16.6	112	47.9	47.9	81	48.8	48.8	81
Ethiopia	27.4	27.4	195	41.4	41.4	88	14.0	14.0	105	14.8	14.8	104
Falkland Islands (Islas Malvinas)	1.0	1.0	133	1.0	1.0	187	(-)	(-)	210	(-)	(-)	210
Faroe Islands	-9.5	-9.5	66	0.1	0.1	208	9.6	9.6	114	13.4	13.4	107
Fiji	-14.5	-14.5	61	4.4	4.4	146	18.9	18.9	101	22.6	22.6	97
Finland	-180.4	-180.4	29	110.2	110.2	64	290.6	290.6	47	301.9	301.9	49
France	-1,051.4	-1,051.4	14	2,243.5	2,243.5	11	3,295.0	3,295.0	9	3,365.4	3,365.4	10
French Guiana	1.3	1.3	138	1.3	1.3	181	0.1	0.1	203	0.1	0.1	204
French Polynesia	4.4	4.4	163	7.1	7.1	132	2.7	2.7	137	2.9	2.9	137
French Southern and Antarctic Lands	0.4	0.4	121	0.4	0.4	199	(-)	(-)	228	(-)	(-)	228
Gabon	3.0	3.0	154	3.7	3.7	152	0.7	0.7	165	0.8	0.8	164
Gambia	5.5	5.5	169	5.5	5.5	139	(-)	(-)	208	(-)	(-)	208
Gaza Strip Administered by Israel	(-)	(-)	107	(-)	(-)	227	(-)	(-)	(X)	(-)	(-)	(X)
Georgia	4.2	4.2	160	22.3	22.3	104	18.1	18.1	102	18.8	18.8	102
Germany	-4,542.1	-4,542.1	3	3,697.3	3,697.3	6	8,239.4	8,239.4	5	8,397.7	8,397.7	5
Ghana	19.5	19.5	185	58.5	58.5	81	39.0	39.0	86	40.4	40.4	86
Gibraltar	77.7	77.7	208	77.7	77.7	73	(-)	(-)	213	(-)	(-)	212
Greece	-44.7	-44.7	49	43.9	43.9	87	88.6	88.6	70	95.6	95.6	69
Greenland	-0.2	-0.2	93	0.2	0.2	207	0.3	0.3	184	0.3	0.3	185
Grenada	4.5	4.5	164	5.0	5.0	140	0.5	0.5	174	0.6	0.6	174
Guadeloupe	10.5	10.5	176	10.7	10.7	125	0.1	0.1	195	0.1	0.1	195
Guatemala*	244.1	244.1	220	526.7	526.7	36	282.6	282.6	49	310.0	310.0	47
Guinea	0.8	0.8	128	3.7	3.7	154	2.9	2.9	136	3.9	3.9	133
Guinea-Bissau	0.1	0.1	113	0.1	0.1	212	(-)	(-)	(X)	(-)	(-)	(X)
Guyana	52.1	52.1	203	86.5	86.5	70	34.4	34.4	88	34.9	34.9	88
Haiti	22.0	22.0	189	71.7	71.7	76	49.7	49.7	80	50.7	50.7	80
Heard and McDonald Islands	(-)	(-)	(X)	(-)	(-)	(X)	(-)	(-)	(X)	(-)	(-)	(X)
Honduras**	115.2	115.2	214	398.7	398.7	39	283.5	283.5	48	306.9	306.9	48
Hong Kong	2,188.5	2,188.5	233	2,673.0	2,673.0	8	484.6	484.6	38	495.9	495.9	38
Hungary	-276.6	-276.6	24	154.1	154.1	56	430.7	430.7	40	437.0	437.0	40
Iceland	0.7	0.7	127	26.6	26.6	98	25.8	25.8	94	27.6	27.6	93
India	-2,191.5	-2,191.5	9	1,488.7	1,488.7	17	3,680.1	3,680.1	7	3,808.6	3,808.6	7
Indonesia	-828.5	-828.5	15	731.1	731.1	29	1,559.6	1,559.6	19	1,641.0	1,641.0	19
Iran	10.2	10.2	175	10.2	10.2	126	(-)	(-)	(X)	(-)	(-)	(X)
Iraq	-106.3	-106.3	38	95.7	95.7	67	202.1	202.1	58	214.4	214.4	58
Ireland	-2,389.5	-2,389.5	7	734.3	734.3	28	3,123.9	3,123.9	13	3,136.9	3,136.9	13
Israel*	-806.2	-806.2	16	992.0	992.0	24	1,798.2	1,798.2	17	1,838.4	1,838.4	17
Italy	-1,992.8	-1,992.8	10	1,203.2	1,203.2	20	3,195.9	3,195.9	11	3,287.7	3,287.7	12
Jamaica	90.3	90.3	210	118.1	118.1	62	27.8	27.8	92	29.2	29.2	91
Japan	-4,881.8	-4,881.8	2	4,701.5	4,701.5	4	9,583.3	9,583.3	4	9,809.6	9,809.6	4
Jordan*	21.3	21.3	187	127.7	127.7	61	106.4	106.4	68	109.1	109.1	68
Kazakhstan	-51.9	-51.9	46	25.2	25.2	100	77.1	77.1	72	83.5	83.5	72
Kenya	-13.3	-13.3	62	36.7	36.7	89	49.9	49.9	79	51.8	51.8	79
Kiribati	(-)	(-)	99	(-)	(-)	217	(-)	(-)	205	0.1	0.1	205
Korea, North	(-)	(-)	108	(-)	(-)	222	(-)	(-)	(X)	(-)	(-)	(X)
Korea, South*	-2,724.5	-2,724.5	5	3,187.5	3,187.5	7	5,911.9	5,911.9	6	6,080.6	6,080.6	6
Kosovo	1.3	1.3	139	1.4	1.4	179	0.1	0.1	201	0.1	0.1	201
Kuwait	-29.9	-29.9	53	169.4	169.4	55	199.3	199.3	59	213.5	213.5	59
Kyrgyzstan	-1.6	-1.6	80	0.7	0.7	194	2.3	2.3	141	2.5	2.5	141
Laos	-1.5	-1.5	81	2.0	2.0	173	3.5	3.5	133	3.7	3.7	134
Latvia	-2.9	-2.9	74	20.6	20.6	106	23.5	23.5	96	24.5	24.5	95
Lebanon	68.0	68.0	207	76.3	76.3	74	8.4	8.4	116	8.6	8.6	116
Lesotho	-26.6	-26.6	54	(-)	(-)	228	26.6	26.6	93	27.5	27.5	94
Liberia	3.0	3.0	155	7.5	7.5	130	4.5	4.5	129	4.9	4.9	127
Libya	-6.1	-6.1	67	7.4	7.4	131	13.5	13.5	106	14.1	14.1	106
Liechtenstein	-19.7	-19.7	57	1.3	1.3	182	21.0	21.0	98	21.3	21.3	100
Lithuania	-42.8	-42.8	50	33.4	33.4	92	76.2	76.2	73	80.6	80.6	73
Luxembourg	23.3	23.3	193	64.6	64.6	79	41.3	41.3	85	43.3	43.3	85
Macau	21.9	21.9	188	28.3	28.3	95	6.4	6.4	119	6.6	6.6	120
Macedonia	-11.8	-11.8	64	1.1	1.1	185	13.0	13.0	107	13.2	13.2	109
Madagascar	-19.1	-19.1	58	2.4	2.4	166	21.5	21.5	97	22.0	22.0	98
Malawi	-1.7	-1.7	78	2.2	2.2	170	3.9	3.9	132	4.1	4.1	130

Exhibit 4. Exports, Imports, and Trade Balance of Goods by Country and Area, Not Seasonally Adjusted: 2016

In millions of dollars. Details may not equal totals due to rounding. (X) Not applicable. (-) Represents zero or less than one-half unit of measurement shown.

Country	Balance (Customs imports)			Exports Domestic & Foreign, F.A.S. basis			Imports Customs basis			Imports C.I.F. basis		
	January	Year-to-Date	Rank	January	Year-to-Date	Rank	January	Year-to-Date	Rank	January	Year-to-Date	Rank
Malaysia	-1,544.2	-1,544.2	11	935.1	935.1	25	2,479.4	2,479.4	14	2,535.8	2,535.8	14
Maldives	1.2	1.2	137	3.0	3.0	160	1.8	1.8	149	2.8	2.8	139
Mali	4.8	4.8	165	5.9	5.9	137	1.1	1.1	154	1.1	1.1	154
Malta	-6.0	-6.0	68	6.4	6.4	133	12.4	12.4	108	12.6	12.6	110
Marshall Islands	4.3	4.3	161	4.9	4.9	142	0.6	0.6	171	0.7	0.7	169
Martinique	14.7	14.7	180	14.9	14.9	115	0.1	0.1	194	0.1	0.1	194
Mauritania	11.0	11.0	177	11.0	11.0	124	(-)	(-)	206	(-)	(-)	207
Mauritius	-21.4	-21.4	55	2.4	2.4	167	23.8	23.8	95	24.3	24.3	96
Mayotte	0.6	0.6	125	0.6	0.6	196	(-)	(-)	219	(-)	(-)	219
Mexico**	-4,334.9	-4,334.9	4	18,065.8	18,065.8	2	22,400.7	22,400.7	2	22,642.0	22,642.0	3
Micronesia	2.2	2.2	150	2.3	2.3	169	(-)	(-)	211	(-)	(-)	211
Moldova	-2.2	-2.2	77	0.5	0.5	198	2.6	2.6	138	2.8	2.8	138
Monaco	1.9	1.9	144	4.2	4.2	149	2.3	2.3	140	2.3	2.3	142
Mongolia	1.4	1.4	140	3.4	3.4	158	2.1	2.1	143	2.1	2.1	146
Montenegro	(-)	(-)	101	0.1	0.1	209	0.1	0.1	197	0.1	0.1	196
Montserrat	0.2	0.2	117	0.3	0.3	201	0.1	0.1	202	0.1	0.1	202
Morocco*	50.9	50.9	202	139.5	139.5	58	88.7	88.7	69	93.5	93.5	70
Mozambique	-4.4	-4.4	71	9.7	9.7	128	14.1	14.1	104	14.2	14.2	105
Namibia	8.1	8.1	172	13.4	13.4	119	5.3	5.3	124	5.3	5.3	124
Nauru	(-)	(-)	106	(-)	(-)	225	(-)	(-)	221	(-)	(-)	221
Nepal	-4.9	-4.9	70	1.5	1.5	178	6.4	6.4	120	6.8	6.8	119
Netherlands	1,571.5	1,571.5	232	2,663.1	2,663.1	9	1,091.6	1,091.6	23	1,136.9	1,136.9	23
New Caledonia	0.4	0.4	122	2.4	2.4	164	2.0	2.0	145	2.1	2.1	145
New Zealand	-103.0	-103.0	39	238.4	238.4	47	341.4	341.4	42	356.5	356.5	42
Nicaragua**	-121.5	-121.5	34	97.2	97.2	66	218.7	218.7	56	226.2	226.2	56
Niger	0.7	0.7	126	1.2	1.2	183	0.5	0.5	175	0.5	0.5	176
Nigeria	-47.2	-47.2	48	131.0	131.0	60	178.2	178.2	60	188.0	188.0	60
Niue	-0.1	-0.1	96	(-)	(-)	(X)	0.1	0.1	204	0.1	0.1	203
Norfolk Island	(-)	(-)	109	(-)	(-)	221	(-)	(-)	224	(-)	(-)	224
Norway	-64.2	-64.2	43	272.3	272.3	45	336.5	336.5	43	352.8	352.8	43
Oman*	35.4	35.4	198	85.6	85.6	71	50.2	50.2	78	53.5	53.5	78
Pakistan	-187.2	-187.2	28	95.3	95.3	68	282.5	282.5	50	297.6	297.6	50
Palau	2.2	2.2	148	2.2	2.2	171	(-)	(-)	216	(-)	(-)	216
Panama*	526.8	526.8	227	555.6	555.6	35	28.8	28.8	90	30.0	30.0	90
Papua New Guinea	1.8	1.8	143	8.8	8.8	129	6.9	6.9	117	7.2	7.2	117
Paraguay	94.4	94.4	211	105.9	105.9	65	11.5	11.5	111	12.4	12.4	111
Peru*	197.5	197.5	219	644.9	644.9	32	447.4	447.4	39	484.0	484.0	39
Philippines	-110.0	-110.0	36	609.5	609.5	34	719.5	719.5	30	744.7	744.7	30
Pitcairn Islands	(-)	(-)	105	(-)	(-)	(X)	(-)	(-)	227	(-)	(-)	227
Poland	-135.5	-135.5	31	285.6	285.6	44	421.2	421.2	41	435.4	435.4	41
Portugal	-92.3	-92.3	41	67.1	67.1	77	159.4	159.4	63	166.6	166.6	63
Qatar	98.2	98.2	212	182.0	182.0	53	83.7	83.7	71	86.1	86.1	71
Reunion	-1.3	-1.3	82	0.8	0.8	191	2.1	2.1	142	2.1	2.1	144
Romania	-96.3	-96.3	40	48.7	48.7	84	144.9	144.9	65	151.1	151.1	65
Russia	-597.5	-597.5	18	362.8	362.8	42	960.3	960.3	24	1,017.2	1,017.2	24
Rwanda	-0.8	-0.8	84	0.7	0.7	193	1.5	1.5	151	1.6	1.6	151
Samoa	1.0	1.0	134	1.4	1.4	180	0.4	0.4	178	0.4	0.4	178
San Marino	-0.5	-0.5	88	0.1	0.1	211	0.6	0.6	168	0.7	0.7	168
Sao Tome and Principe	0.2	0.2	116	0.2	0.2	204	(-)	(-)	220	(-)	(-)	220
Saudi Arabia	-352.5	-352.5	22	1,158.8	1,158.8	21	1,511.4	1,511.4	20	1,616.4	1,616.4	20
Senegal	5.0	5.0	166	11.9	11.9	121	6.9	6.9	118	7.1	7.1	118
Serbia	-13.0	-13.0	63	6.0	6.0	136	19.0	19.0	100	19.7	19.7	101
Seychelles	0.6	0.6	124	1.0	1.0	188	0.4	0.4	177	0.4	0.4	177
Sierra Leone	2.9	2.9	153	3.7	3.7	153	0.8	0.8	160	0.9	0.9	161
Singapore*	748.8	748.8	229	2,028.0	2,028.0	14	1,279.2	1,279.2	21	1,295.4	1,295.4	22
Sint Maarten	62.1	62.1	204	74.2	74.2	75	12.1	12.1	109	12.2	12.2	112
Slovakia	-128.9	-128.9	33	26.4	26.4	99	155.3	155.3	64	157.6	157.6	64
Slovenia	-50.8	-50.8	47	11.8	11.8	123	62.6	62.6	74	64.4	64.4	74
Solomon Islands	0.2	0.2	119	0.4	0.4	200	0.1	0.1	198	0.1	0.1	197
Somalia	2.2	2.2	149	2.4	2.4	165	0.2	0.2	189	0.2	0.2	189
South Africa	-260.7	-260.7	25	308.0	308.0	43	568.7	568.7	35	581.8	581.8	36
South Sudan	0.2	0.2	118	0.2	0.2	202	(-)	(-)	218	(-)	(-)	218
Spain	-83.8	-83.8	42	846.8	846.8	26	930.5	930.5	25	972.3	972.3	25
Sri Lanka	-205.1	-205.1	26	28.9	28.9	94	233.9	233.9	53	244.3	244.3	54
St Helena	-0.5	-0.5	87	(-)	(-)	226	0.6	0.6	172	0.6	0.6	172

Exhibit 4. Exports, Imports, and Trade Balance of Goods by Country and Area, Not Seasonally Adjusted: 2016

In millions of dollars. Details may not equal totals due to rounding. (X) Not applicable. (-) Represents zero or less than one-half unit of measurement shown.

Country	Balance (Customs imports)			Exports Domestic & Foreign, F.A.S. basis			Imports Customs basis			Imports C.I.F. basis		
	January	Year-to-Date	Rank	January	Year-to-Date	Rank	January	Year-to-Date	Rank	January	Year-to-Date	Rank
St Kitts and Nevis	9.5	9.5	174	13.5	13.5	117	3.9	3.9	131	4.1	4.1	131
St Lucia	18.9	18.9	184	20.1	20.1	107	1.2	1.2	153	1.3	1.3	153
St Pierre and Miquelon	(-)	(-)	104	(-)	(-)	(X)	(-)	(-)	226	(-)	(-)	226
St Vincent and the Grenadines	5.7	5.7	170	5.9	5.9	138	0.2	0.2	192	0.2	0.2	192
Sudan	3.1	3.1	156	4.0	4.0	151	0.9	0.9	158	1.0	1.0	158
Suriname	17.6	17.6	183	22.5	22.5	103	4.9	4.9	125	5.1	5.1	126
Svalbard, Jan Mayen Island	(-)	(-)	103	(-)	(-)	(X)	(-)	(-)	225	(-)	(-)	225
Swaziland	1.7	1.7	142	2.0	2.0	174	0.3	0.3	181	0.4	0.4	182
Sweden	-460.3	-460.3	21	238.4	238.4	46	698.7	698.7	32	716.4	716.4	32
Switzerland	-698.3	-698.3	17	1,466.3	1,466.3	18	2,164.6	2,164.6	16	2,184.5	2,184.5	16
Syria	0.1	0.1	112	0.6	0.6	197	0.5	0.5	176	0.5	0.5	175
Taiwan	-1,120.6	-1,120.6	13	2,131.8	2,131.8	12	3,252.3	3,252.3	10	3,374.2	3,374.2	9
Tajikistan	1.1	1.1	136	1.1	1.1	184	(-)	(-)	212	(-)	(-)	213
Tanzania	-16.8	-16.8	60	11.8	11.8	122	28.6	28.6	91	29.0	29.0	92
Thailand	-1,451.7	-1,451.7	12	742.1	742.1	27	2,193.9	2,193.9	15	2,268.3	2,268.3	15
Timor-Leste	(-)	(-)	98	0.2	0.2	205	0.2	0.2	191	0.2	0.2	190
Togo	5.3	5.3	168	6.2	6.2	135	0.9	0.9	159	0.9	0.9	159
Tokelau	-0.1	-0.1	95	(-)	(-)	220	0.1	0.1	196	0.1	0.1	198
Tonga	0.9	0.9	131	1.1	1.1	186	0.2	0.2	188	0.4	0.4	179
Trinidad and Tobago	-116.8	-116.8	35	192.2	192.2	50	309.0	309.0	45	327.3	327.3	44
Tunisia	0.8	0.8	129	33.8	33.8	90	32.9	32.9	89	33.8	33.8	89
Turkey	65.9	65.9	206	720.6	720.6	30	654.7	654.7	34	695.3	695.3	34
Turkmenistan	3.6	3.6	158	4.3	4.3	148	0.7	0.7	166	0.7	0.7	166
Turks and Caicos Islands	21.1	21.1	186	21.4	21.4	105	0.3	0.3	183	0.3	0.3	184
Tuvalu	(-)	(-)	111	0.1	0.1	215	(-)	(-)	222	(-)	(-)	222
Uganda	-2.2	-2.2	76	3.5	3.5	155	5.7	5.7	121	6.0	6.0	121
Ukraine	23.1	23.1	192	66.1	66.1	78	42.9	42.9	83	44.9	44.9	83
United Arab Emirates	1,427.0	1,427.0	231	1,659.4	1,659.4	15	232.4	232.4	54	244.4	244.4	53
United Kingdom	270.8	270.8	222	3,919.9	3,919.9	5	3,649.1	3,649.1	8	3,720.2	3,720.2	8
Uruguay	50.4	50.4	201	93.2	93.2	69	42.8	42.8	84	44.0	44.0	84
Uzbekistan	1.9	1.9	146	2.9	2.9	163	1.0	1.0	157	1.0	1.0	157
Vanuatu	2.2	2.2	147	2.3	2.3	168	0.1	0.1	199	0.1	0.1	199
Vatican City	(-)	(-)	110	(-)	(-)	219	(-)	(-)	217	(-)	(-)	217
Venezuela	-276.6	-276.6	23	389.0	389.0	40	665.7	665.7	33	716.5	716.5	31
Vietnam	-2,548.7	-2,548.7	6	622.5	622.5	33	3,171.2	3,171.2	12	3,306.6	3,306.6	11
Wallis and Futuna	(-)	(-)	102	(-)	(-)	224	(-)	(-)	215	(-)	(-)	215
West Bank Administered by Israel	-0.6	-0.6	86	0.1	0.1	213	0.7	0.7	167	0.8	0.8	165
Western Sahara	(-)	(-)	97	(-)	(-)	(X)	(-)	(-)	209	(-)	(-)	209
Yemen	3.2	3.2	157	3.4	3.4	157	0.3	0.3	186	0.3	0.3	188
Zambia	0.9	0.9	132	4.9	4.9	141	4.0	4.0	130	4.1	4.1	132
Zimbabwe	1.0	1.0	135	1.8	1.8	175	0.7	0.7	163	0.8	0.8	162
Unidentified (1)	(-)	(-)	(X)	(-)	(-)	(X)	(-)	(-)	(X)	(-)	(-)	(X)
Timing adjustment	(-)	(-)	(X)	(-)	(-)	(X)	(-)	(-)	(X)	(-)	(-)	(X)

Exhibit 4. Exports, Imports, and Trade Balance of Goods by Country and Area, Not Seasonally Adjusted: 2016

In millions of dollars. Details may not equal totals due to rounding. (X) Not applicable. (-) Represents zero or less than one-half unit of measurement shown.

Country	Balance (Customs imports)			Exports Domestic & Foreign, F.A.S. basis			Imports Customs basis			Imports C.I.F. basis		
	January	Year-to-Date	Rank	January	Year-to-Date	Rank	January	Year-to-Date	Rank	January	Year-to-Date	Rank
Africa	-357.5	-357.5	(X)	1,523.1	1,523.1	(X)	1,880.6	1,880.6	(X)	1,960.8	1,960.8	(X)
APEC	-47,265.2	-47,265.2	(X)	68,472.7	68,472.7	(X)	115,737.9	115,737.9	(X)	119,258.6	119,258.6	(X)
ASEAN	-5,920.5	-5,920.5	(X)	5,728.8	5,728.8	(X)	11,649.3	11,649.3	(X)	12,047.3	12,047.3	(X)
Asia - South	-2,919.2	-2,919.2	(X)	1,833.8	1,833.8	(X)	4,753.0	4,753.0	(X)	4,926.3	4,926.3	(X)
Asia Near East	364.7	364.7	(X)	4,618.2	4,618.2	(X)	4,253.6	4,253.6	(X)	4,447.8	4,447.8	(X)
CAFTA-DR	716.4	716.4	(X)	2,201.6	2,201.6	(X)	1,485.2	1,485.2	(X)	1,572.6	1,572.6	(X)
Central American Common Market	451.7	451.7	(X)	1,693.3	1,693.3	(X)	1,241.6	1,241.6	(X)	1,323.0	1,323.0	(X)
Euro Area	-7,390.0	-7,390.0	(X)	15,456.6	15,456.6	(X)	22,846.6	22,846.6	(X)	23,357.8	23,357.8	(X)
Europe	-10,106.1	-10,106.1	(X)	23,552.6	23,552.6	(X)	33,658.8	33,658.8	(X)	34,460.7	34,460.7	(X)
European Union	-8,832.6	-8,832.6	(X)	20,455.1	20,455.1	(X)	29,287.7	29,287.7	(X)	29,938.8	29,938.8	(X)
LAFTA	-3,112.8	-3,112.8	(X)	24,779.9	24,779.9	(X)	27,892.7	27,892.7	(X)	28,512.5	28,512.5	(X)
NATO Allies	-8,495.2	-8,495.2	(X)	39,077.6	39,077.6	(X)	47,572.8	47,572.8	(X)	48,784.5	48,784.5	(X)
NICs	-907.7	-907.7	(X)	10,020.3	10,020.3	(X)	10,928.0	10,928.0	(X)	11,246.0	11,246.0	(X)
North America	-6,700.2	-6,700.2	(X)	37,864.7	37,864.7	(X)	44,564.9	44,564.9	(X)	45,368.1	45,368.1	(X)
OECD	-22,967.0	-22,967.0	(X)	70,275.8	70,275.8	(X)	93,242.8	93,242.8	(X)	95,193.5	95,193.5	(X)
OPEC	-364.4	-364.4	(X)	5,216.9	5,216.9	(X)	5,581.2	5,581.2	(X)	5,946.2	5,946.2	(X)
Pacific Rim Countries	-36,583.1	-36,583.1	(X)	27,013.0	27,013.0	(X)	63,596.1	63,596.1	(X)	65,927.3	65,927.3	(X)
South/Central America	3,098.0	3,098.0	(X)	10,596.8	10,596.8	(X)	7,498.8	7,498.8	(X)	7,989.1	7,989.1	(X)
Twenty Latin American Republics	-1,824.6	-1,824.6	(X)	27,631.9	27,631.9	(X)	29,456.5	29,456.5	(X)	30,165.8	30,165.8	(X)

* Countries denoted by asterisks represent countries with Free Trade Agreements with the United States.
** Countries denoted by double asterisks represent countries included within Free Trade Agreements with the United States.

Africa - Algeria, Angola, Benin, Botswana, British Indian Ocean Territories, Burkina Faso, Burundi, Cameroon, Cabo Verde, Central African Republic, Chad, Comoros, Congo (Brazzaville), Congo (Kinshasa), Cote d'Ivoire, Djibouti, Egypt, Equatorial Guinea, Eritrea, Ethiopia, French Southern and Antarctic Lands, Gabon, Gambia, Ghana, Guinea, Guinea-Bissau, Kenya, Lesotho, Liberia, Libya, Madagascar, Malawi, Mali, Mauritania, Mauritius, Mayotte, Morocco, Mozambique, Namibia, Niger, Nigeria, Reunion, Rwanda, Sao Tome and Principe, Senegal, Seychelles, Sierra Leone, Somalia, South Africa, South Sudan, St. Helena, Sudan, Swaziland, Tanzania, Togo, Tunisia, Uganda, Western Sahara, Zambia, Zimbabwe.

APEC (Asia - Pacific Economic Cooperation) - Australia, Brunei, Canada, Chile, China, Hong Kong, Indonesia, Japan, Korea (South), Malaysia, Mexico, New Zealand, Papua New Guinea, Peru, Philippines, Russia, Singapore, Taiwan, Thailand, Vietnam.

ASEAN (Association of Southeast Asian Nations) - Brunei, Burma, Cambodia, Indonesia, Laos, Malaysia, Philippines, Singapore, Thailand, Vietnam.

Asia - South - Afghanistan, Bangladesh, India, Nepal, Pakistan, Sri Lanka.

Asia Near East - Bahrain, Gaza Strip Administered by Israel, Iran, Iraq, Israel, Jordan, Kuwait, Lebanon, Oman, Qatar, Saudi Arabia, Syria, United Arab Emirates, West Bank Administered by Israel, Yemen.

CAFTA-DR (Dominican Republic-Central America-United States Free Trade Agreement) - Costa Rica, Dominican Republic, El Salvador, Guatemala, Honduras, Nicaragua.

Central American Common Market - Costa Rica, El Salvador, Guatemala, Honduras, Nicaragua.

Euro Area - Austria, Belgium, Cyprus, Estonia, Finland, France, Germany, Greece, Ireland, taly, Latvia, Lithuania, Luxembourg, Malta, Netherlands, Portugal, Slovakia, Slovenia, Spain.

Europe - Albania, Andorra, Armenia, Austria, Azerbaijan, Belarus, Belgium, Bosnia-Herzegovina, Bulgaria, Croatia, Cyprus, Czech Republic, Denmark, Estonia, Faroe Islands, Finland, France, Georgia, Germany, Gibraltar, Greece, Hungary, Iceland, Ireland, taly, Kazakhstan, Kosovo, Kyrgyzstan, Latvia, Liechtenstein, Lithuania, Luxembourg, Macedonia, Malta, Moldova, Monaco, Montenegro, Netherlands, Norway, Poland, Portugal, Romania, Russia, San Marino, Serbia, Slovakia, Slovenia, Spain, Svalbard, Jan Mayen Island, Sweden, Switzerland, Tajikistan, Turkey, Turkmenistan, Ukraine, United Kingdom, Uzbekistan, Vatican City.

European Union - Austria, Belgium, Bulgaria, Croatia, Cyprus, Czech Republic, Denmark, Estonia, Finland, France, Germany, Greece, Hungary, Ireland, Italy, Latvia, Lithuania, Luxembourg, Malta, Netherlands, Poland, Portugal, Romania, Slovakia, Slovenia, Spain, Sweden, United Kingdom.

LAFTA (Latin American Free Trade Area) - Argentina, Bolivia, Brazil, Chile, Colombia, Ecuador, Mexico, Paraguay, Peru, Uruguay, Venezuela.

NATO (North Atlantic Treaty Organization) Allies - Belgium, Bulgaria, Canada, Czech Republic, Denmark, Estonia, France, Germany, Greece, Hungary, Iceland, Italy, Latvia, Lithuania, Luxembourg, Netherlands, Norway, Poland, Portugal, Romania, Slovakia, Slovenia, Spain, Turkey, United Kingdom.

NICs (Newly Industrialized Countries) - Hong Kong, Korea (South), Singapore, Taiwan.

North America - Canada, Mexico.

OECD (Organization for Economic Cooperation and Development) - Australia, Austria, Belgium, Canada, Chile, Czech Republic, Denmark, Estonia, Finland, France, Germany, Greece, Hungary, Iceland, Ireland, Israel, Italy, Japan, Korea (South), Luxembourg, Mexico, Netherlands, New Zealand, Norway, Poland, Portugal, Slovakia, Slovenia, Spain, Sweden, Switzerland, Turkey, United Kingdom.

OPEC (Organization of the Petroleum Exporting Countries) - Algeria, Angola, Ecuador, Indonesia, Iran, Iraq, Kuwait, Libya, Nigeria, Qatar, Saudi Arabia, United Arab Emirates, Venezuela.

Pacific Rim Countries - Australia, Brunei, China, Hong Kong, Indonesia, Japan, Korea (South), Macau, Malaysia, New Zealand, Papua New Guinea, Philippines, Singapore, Taiwan.

South/Central America - Anguilla, Antigua and Barbuda, Argentina, Aruba, Bahamas, Barbados, Belize, Bermuda, Bolivia, Brazil, British Virgin Islands, Cayman Islands, Chile, Colombia, Costa Rica, Cuba, Curacao, Dominica, Dominican Republic, Ecuador, El Salvador, Falkland Islands (Islas Malvinas), French Guiana, Grenada, Guadeloupe, Guatemala, Guyana, Haiti, Honduras, Jamaica, Martinique, Montserrat, Nicaragua, Panama, Paraguay, Peru, St. Kitts and Nevis, Sint Maarten, St. Lucia, St. Vincent and the Grenadines, Suriname, Trinidad and Tobago, Turks and Caicos Islands, Uruguay, Venezuela.

Twenty Latin American Republics - Argentina, Bolivia, Brazil, Chile, Colombia, Costa Rica, Cuba, Dominican Republic, Ecuador, El Salvador, Guatemala, Haiti, Honduras, Mexico, Nicaragua, Panama, Paraguay, Peru, Uruguay, Venezuela.

(1) The export totals reflect shipments of certain grains, oilseeds, and satellites that are not included in the country/area totals.
NOTE: Area data reflect the composition of the areas at the time of reporting.

Exhibit 4a. Exports, Imports, and Trade Balance of Goods by Country and Area, Not Seasonally Adjusted: 2015

In millions of dollars. Details may not equal totals due to rounding. (X) Not applicable. (-) Represents zero or less than one-half unit of measurement shown.

Country	Balance (Customs imports)			Exports Domestic & Foreign, F.A.S. basis			Imports Customs basis			Imports C.I.F. basis		
	January	Year-to-Date	Rank	January	Year-to-Date	Rank	January	Year-to-Date	Rank	January	Year-to-Date	Rank
TOTAL	**-58,715.5**	**-58,715.5**	**(X)**	**121,397.9**	**121,397.9**	**(X)**	**180,113.5**	**180,113.5**	**(X)**	**185,571.3**	**185,571.3**	**(X)**
Afghanistan	34.8	34.8	192	36.4	36.4	97	1.6	1.6	152	1.7	1.7	152
Albania	-22.5	-22.5	56	2.1	2.1	174	24.6	24.6	99	24.7	24.7	100
Algeria	-121.6	-121.6	38	148.8	148.8	61	270.4	270.4	54	284.4	284.4	54
Andorra	(-)	(-)	115	0.1	0.1	214	0.1	0.1	201	0.1	0.1	201
Angola	-81.9	-81.9	45	79.5	79.5	80	161.3	161.3	63	165.8	165.8	63
Anguilla	1.8	1.8	143	2.5	2.5	166	0.7	0.7	168	0.7	0.7	169
Antigua and Barbuda	74.3	74.3	202	74.6	74.6	81	0.3	0.3	185	0.3	0.3	186
Argentina	324.5	324.5	225	687.3	687.3	33	362.8	362.8	48	382.3	382.3	47
Armenia	-1.7	-1.7	86	3.1	3.1	162	4.8	4.8	134	5.0	5.0	134
Aruba	120.4	120.4	208	121.5	121.5	69	1.2	1.2	158	1.2	1.2	159
Australia*	1,097.6	1,097.6	229	1,975.2	1,975.2	14	877.6	877.6	30	905.1	905.1	30
Austria	-39.4	-39.4	50	791.2	791.2	28	830.6	830.6	32	849.6	849.6	32
Azerbaijan	18.4	18.4	184	22.5	22.5	115	4.1	4.1	139	4.3	4.3	139
Bahamas	139.6	139.6	212	170.8	170.8	58	31.2	31.2	92	34.4	34.4	91
Bahrain*	-3.1	-3.1	78	99.9	99.9	72	103.1	103.1	73	108.4	108.4	73
Bangladesh	-457.5	-457.5	22	30.4	30.4	101	487.9	487.9	40	506.5	506.5	40
Barbados	59.3	59.3	199	61.7	61.7	87	2.4	2.4	148	2.5	2.5	148
Belarus	-13.1	-13.1	63	2.6	2.6	164	15.7	15.7	109	16.7	16.7	109
Belgium	1,513.0	1,513.0	230	2,878.4	2,878.4	9	1,365.4	1,365.4	24	1,404.1	1,404.1	24
Belize	15.0	15.0	180	19.2	19.2	120	4.2	4.2	138	4.6	4.6	136
Benin	65.9	65.9	201	66.7	66.7	84	0.7	0.7	167	0.7	0.7	167
Bermuda	64.9	64.9	200	69.4	69.4	83	4.5	4.5	135	4.5	4.5	137
Bhutan	0.1	0.1	121	0.1	0.1	209	(-)	(-)	218	(-)	(-)	218
Bolivia	-58.0	-58.0	47	66.6	66.6	85	124.6	124.6	67	125.3	125.3	68
Bosnia and Herzegovina	-4.7	-4.7	76	1.7	1.7	178	6.3	6.3	126	6.5	6.5	128
Botswana	-2.4	-2.4	84	3.8	3.8	157	6.1	6.1	127	6.5	6.5	129
Brazil	367.4	367.4	226	2,833.4	2,833.4	11	2,466.0	2,466.0	15	2,551.3	2,551.3	15
British Indian Ocean Territories	-0.5	-0.5	95	(-)	(-)	225	0.5	0.5	177	0.5	0.5	177
British Virgin Islands	12.6	12.6	177	13.5	13.5	127	1.0	1.0	162	1.0	1.0	162
Brunei	8.2	8.2	171	9.7	9.7	140	1.5	1.5	153	1.6	1.6	153
Bulgaria	-17.4	-17.4	59	25.3	25.3	112	42.6	42.6	87	44.5	44.5	86
Burkina Faso	1.9	1.9	144	2.2	2.2	170	0.3	0.3	180	0.4	0.4	181
Burma	5.2	5.2	163	14.2	14.2	126	8.9	8.9	121	9.3	9.3	121
Burundi	-0.4	-0.4	98	0.6	0.6	192	0.9	0.9	163	0.9	0.9	164
Cabo Verde	-0.1	-0.1	102	0.3	0.3	197	0.4	0.4	178	0.4	0.4	178
Cambodia	-205.0	-205.0	31	25.8	25.8	109	230.8	230.8	57	239.8	239.8	57
Cameroon	5.6	5.6	165	14.8	14.8	125	9.2	9.2	120	9.9	9.9	120
Canada**	-2,941.3	-2,941.3	5	22,463.6	22,463.6	1	25,404.9	25,404.9	2	26,005.3	26,005.3	2
Cayman Islands	46.6	46.6	197	48.0	48.0	92	1.4	1.4	154	1.5	1.5	154
Central African Republic	0.2	0.2	125	0.2	0.2	205	(-)	(-)	204	(-)	(-)	204
Chad	-111.9	-111.9	39	8.7	8.7	143	120.6	120.6	69	122.5	122.5	70
Chile*	191.4	191.4	219	1,167.6	1,167.6	22	976.3	976.3	28	1,061.0	1,061.0	28
China	-28,606.4	-28,606.4	1	9,552.0	9,552.0	3	38,158.4	38,158.4	1	39,808.3	39,808.3	1
Christmas Island	(-)	(-)	114	0.2	0.2	204	0.2	0.2	190	0.2	0.2	190
Cocos (Keeling) Islands	-0.1	-0.1	103	(-)	(-)	(X)	0.1	0.1	202	0.1	0.1	202
Colombia*	151.5	151.5	217	1,379.1	1,379.1	20	1,227.6	1,227.6	26	1,280.7	1,280.7	26
Comoros	-0.1	-0.1	101	0.1	0.1	220	0.1	0.1	194	0.1	0.1	194
Congo (Brazzaville)	-47.5	-47.5	49	18.6	18.6	121	66.1	66.1	78	68.9	68.9	78
Congo (Kinshasa)	-4.7	-4.7	75	9.1	9.1	141	13.9	13.9	112	14.0	14.0	112
Cook Islands	0.2	0.2	124	0.3	0.3	198	0.2	0.2	192	0.2	0.2	192
Costa Rica**	143.5	143.5	215	511.5	511.5	39	368.0	368.0	46	385.6	385.6	46
Cote d'Ivoire	-82.7	-82.7	44	26.3	26.3	107	108.9	108.9	72	113.6	113.6	72
Croatia	-7.3	-7.3	72	29.7	29.7	102	37.0	37.0	88	38.0	38.0	88
Cuba	25.3	25.3	189	25.3	25.3	111	(-)	(-)	(X)	(-)	(-)	(X)
Curacao	17.7	17.7	183	26.1	26.1	108	8.4	8.4	122	8.5	8.5	123
Cyprus	3.7	3.7	153	7.1	7.1	145	3.5	3.5	143	3.6	3.6	143
Czech Republic	-204.6	-204.6	32	173.7	173.7	57	378.3	378.3	45	389.8	389.8	45
Denmark	-420.8	-420.8	24	195.7	195.7	53	616.5	616.5	37	625.1	625.1	37
Djibouti	2.0	2.0	145	13.3	13.3	129	11.3	11.3	116	11.3	11.3	117
Dominica	5.4	5.4	164	5.5	5.5	150	0.1	0.1	195	0.1	0.1	196
Dominican Republic**	324.3	324.3	224	578.8	578.8	37	254.6	254.6	56	262.1	262.1	56
Ecuador	-440.5	-440.5	23	466.6	466.6	42	907.1	907.1	29	959.1	959.1	29
Egypt	237.6	237.6	222	357.5	357.5	44	119.9	119.9	70	125.7	125.7	67
El Salvador**	75.9	75.9	203	244.1	244.1	48	168.2	168.2	62	173.4	173.4	62
Equatorial Guinea	11.5	11.5	176	12.0	12.0	132	0.5	0.5	175	0.5	0.5	175
Eritrea	0.1	0.1	119	0.1	0.1	210	(-)	(-)	210	(-)	(-)	210

Exhibit 4a. Exports, Imports, and Trade Balance of Goods by Country and Area, Not Seasonally Adjusted: 2015

In millions of dollars. Details may not equal totals due to rounding. (X) Not applicable. (-) Represents zero or less than one-half unit of measurement shown.

Country	Balance (Customs imports)			Exports Domestic & Foreign, F.A.S. basis			Imports Customs basis			Imports C.I.F. basis		
	January	Year-to-Date	Rank	January	Year-to-Date	Rank	January	Year-to-Date	Rank	January	Year-to-Date	Rank
Estonia	-9.4	-9.4	68	26.4	26.4	106	35.8	35.8	89	36.7	36.7	89
Ethiopia	135.1	135.1	210	145.3	145.3	63	10.2	10.2	118	10.6	10.6	118
Falkland Islands (Islas Malvinas)	-1.0	-1.0	92	0.1	0.1	211	1.1	1.1	160	1.1	1.1	161
Faroe Islands	-4.8	-4.8	74	0.1	0.1	213	4.9	4.9	133	6.7	6.7	127
Fiji	-10.8	-10.8	66	5.0	5.0	153	15.8	15.8	108	19.6	19.6	105
Finland	-265.1	-265.1	28	156.7	156.7	60	421.9	421.9	42	436.6	436.6	41
France	-924.1	-924.1	17	2,577.1	2,577.1	12	3,501.2	3,501.2	9	3,558.9	3,558.9	9
French Guiana	1.0	1.0	135	1.0	1.0	188	(-)	(-)	217	(-)	(-)	217
French Polynesia	6.9	6.9	168	10.7	10.7	136	3.7	3.7	142	3.9	3.9	142
French Southern and Antarctic Lands	1.1	1.1	137	1.1	1.1	187	(-)	(-)	(X)	(-)	(-)	(X)
Gabon	5.2	5.2	162	18.0	18.0	123	12.8	12.8	113	13.7	13.7	113
Gambia	2.3	2.3	149	2.3	2.3	168	(-)	(-)	211	(-)	(-)	212
Gaza Strip Administered by Israel	(-)	(-)	116	(-)	(-)	221	(-)	(-)	(X)	(-)	(-)	(X)
Georgia	7.1	7.1	169	33.3	33.3	98	26.3	26.3	96	27.6	27.6	96
Germany	-5,298.1	-5,298.1	3	3,743.7	3,743.7	6	9,041.8	9,041.8	5	9,218.6	9,218.6	5
Ghana	39.5	39.5	195	55.4	55.4	90	15.9	15.9	107	17.2	17.2	108
Gibraltar	185.6	185.6	218	185.6	185.6	54	(-)	(-)	209	(-)	(-)	209
Greece	-24.9	-24.9	54	71.1	71.1	82	96.0	96.0	75	101.4	101.4	75
Greenland	0.2	0.2	126	0.3	0.3	202	0.1	0.1	198	0.1	0.1	198
Grenada	10.0	10.0	173	10.5	10.5	138	0.5	0.5	176	0.5	0.5	176
Guadeloupe	21.8	21.8	186	21.9	21.9	118	0.1	0.1	197	0.1	0.1	197
Guatemala*	142.6	142.6	214	474.1	474.1	41	331.5	331.5	50	360.3	360.3	50
Guinea	-2.6	-2.6	83	3.2	3.2	160	5.7	5.7	130	8.5	8.5	124
Guinea-Bissau	0.2	0.2	123	0.2	0.2	207	(-)	(-)	220	(-)	(-)	220
Guyana	-13.3	-13.3	62	22.3	22.3	116	35.6	35.6	90	36.1	36.1	90
Haiti	35.1	35.1	193	84.0	84.0	78	49.0	49.0	82	49.9	49.9	82
Heard and McDonald Islands	(-)	(-)	109	(-)	(-)	227	(-)	(-)	219	(-)	(-)	219
Honduras**	139.9	139.9	213	444.1	444.1	43	304.2	304.2	51	326.9	326.9	51
Hong Kong	2,497.0	2,497.0	233	2,863.2	2,863.2	10	366.2	366.2	47	376.1	376.1	48
Hungary	-291.5	-291.5	27	134.9	134.9	67	426.4	426.4	41	433.7	433.7	42
Iceland	2.7	2.7	151	28.8	28.8	103	26.1	26.1	97	27.6	27.6	97
India	-2,089.0	-2,089.0	9	1,544.0	1,544.0	18	3,633.0	3,633.0	8	3,784.3	3,784.3	8
Indonesia	-1,078.5	-1,078.5	14	579.5	579.5	36	1,658.0	1,658.0	20	1,740.9	1,740.9	20
Iran	13.3	13.3	178	13.3	13.3	130	(-)	(-)	(X)	(-)	(-)	(X)
Iraq	-178.0	-178.0	33	243.4	243.4	49	421.4	421.4	43	432.9	432.9	43
Ireland	-2,355.7	-2,355.7	7	621.2	621.2	35	2,976.9	2,976.9	12	2,987.8	2,987.8	12
Israel*	-1,030.1	-1,030.1	15	1,067.9	1,067.9	23	2,098.0	2,098.0	19	2,142.7	2,142.7	19
Italy	-2,021.2	-2,021.2	10	1,221.1	1,221.1	21	3,242.3	3,242.3	10	3,333.8	3,333.8	10
Jamaica	116.5	116.5	207	138.7	138.7	66	22.2	22.2	103	24.0	24.0	102
Japan	-5,766.0	-5,766.0	2	5,116.7	5,116.7	4	10,882.7	10,882.7	4	11,176.9	11,176.9	4
Jordan*	-2.6	-2.6	81	119.1	119.1	70	121.8	121.8	68	124.6	124.6	69
Kazakhstan	-53.2	-53.2	48	43.6	43.6	95	96.8	96.8	74	102.0	102.0	74
Kenya	35.2	35.2	194	87.8	87.8	77	52.6	52.6	80	54.8	54.8	80
Kiribati	2.2	2.2	148	2.6	2.6	165	0.3	0.3	181	0.4	0.4	180
Korea, North	0.1	0.1	122	0.1	0.1	208	(-)	(-)	(X)	(-)	(-)	(X)
Korea, South*	-3,067.7	-3,067.7	4	3,318.5	3,318.5	7	6,386.2	6,386.2	6	6,611.6	6,611.6	6
Kosovo	0.4	0.4	130	0.4	0.4	196	(-)	(-)	203	(-)	(-)	203
Kuwait	-530.1	-530.1	20	181.6	181.6	55	711.8	711.8	35	734.8	734.8	33
Kyrgyzstan	5.1	5.1	160	5.2	5.2	152	0.1	0.1	199	0.1	0.1	199
Laos	-1.2	-1.2	90	2.6	2.6	163	3.8	3.8	141	4.0	4.0	141
Latvia	-1.5	-1.5	87	21.9	21.9	117	23.4	23.4	101	24.6	24.6	101
Lebanon	136.4	136.4	211	140.8	140.8	64	4.4	4.4	137	4.7	4.7	135
Lesotho	-24.6	-24.6	55	0.1	0.1	215	24.7	24.7	98	25.6	25.6	98
Liberia	6.9	6.9	167	10.8	10.8	134	3.9	3.9	140	4.0	4.0	140
Libya	-4.7	-4.7	77	18.5	18.5	122	23.2	23.2	102	23.5	23.5	103
Liechtenstein	-22.2	-22.2	57	2.2	2.2	172	24.4	24.4	100	24.7	24.7	99
Lithuania	-12.1	-12.1	65	45.4	45.4	93	57.5	57.5	79	61.3	61.3	79
Luxembourg	10.1	10.1	175	55.6	55.6	89	45.5	45.5	84	46.7	46.7	84
Macau	20.9	20.9	185	26.7	26.7	105	5.9	5.9	129	6.0	6.0	131
Macedonia	-13.9	-13.9	61	0.6	0.6	191	14.4	14.4	110	14.9	14.9	110
Madagascar	-9.9	-9.9	67	9.7	9.7	139	19.6	19.6	104	20.1	20.1	104
Malawi	-2.6	-2.6	80	2.3	2.3	169	4.9	4.9	132	5.1	5.1	133

Exhibit 4a. Exports, Imports, and Trade Balance of Goods by Country and Area, Not Seasonally Adjusted: 2015

In millions of dollars. Details may not equal totals due to rounding. (X) Not applicable. (-) Represents zero or less than one-half unit of measurement shown.

Country	Balance (Customs imports)			Exports Domestic & Foreign, F.A.S. basis			Imports Customs basis			Imports C.I.F. basis		
	January	Year-to-Date	Rank	January	Year-to-Date	Rank	January	Year-to-Date	Rank	January	Year-to-Date	Rank
Malaysia	-1,620.0	-1,620.0	11	966.4	966.4	25	2,586.4	2,586.4	14	2,643.4	2,643.4	14
Maldives	(-)	(-)	110	2.2	2.2	173	2.2	2.2	149	3.5	3.5	144
Mali	2.5	2.5	150	3.2	3.2	161	0.6	0.6	171	0.6	0.6	171
Malta	52.2	52.2	198	63.9	63.9	86	11.7	11.7	115	12.0	12.0	114
Marshall Islands	2.1	2.1	146	3.2	3.2	159	1.1	1.1	161	1.4	1.4	156
Martinique	17.6	17.6	182	25.6	25.6	110	8.0	8.0	123	8.6	8.6	122
Mauritania	6.0	6.0	166	6.2	6.2	146	0.2	0.2	189	0.2	0.2	189
Mauritius	-26.8	-26.8	53	1.7	1.7	179	28.4	28.4	94	29.1	29.1	94
Mayotte	0.6	0.6	132	0.6	0.6	190	(-)	(-)	(X)	(-)	(-)	(X)
Mexico**	-2,918.2	-2,918.2	6	19,143.5	19,143.5	2	22,061.7	22,061.7	3	22,294.9	22,294.9	3
Micronesia	2.2	2.2	147	2.2	2.2	171	(-)	(-)	207	(-)	(-)	207
Moldova	-1.3	-1.3	88	1.3	1.3	183	2.6	2.6	146	2.8	2.8	146
Monaco	0.1	0.1	120	1.9	1.9	175	1.8	1.8	151	1.8	1.8	151
Mongolia	4.4	4.4	156	5.8	5.8	149	1.3	1.3	156	1.4	1.4	157
Montenegro	0.3	0.3	128	0.5	0.5	194	0.3	0.3	186	0.3	0.3	187
Montserrat	0.2	0.2	127	0.5	0.5	195	0.3	0.3	188	0.3	0.3	188
Morocco*	133.4	133.4	209	202.3	202.3	52	68.9	68.9	76	76.4	76.4	76
Mozambique	4.2	4.2	155	23.1	23.1	114	18.9	18.9	105	19.0	19.0	106
Namibia	7.9	7.9	170	10.6	10.6	137	2.7	2.7	145	2.7	2.7	147
Nauru	(-)	(-)	107	(-)	(-)	226	(-)	(-)	212	(-)	(-)	213
Nepal	-8.3	-8.3	71	1.3	1.3	182	9.6	9.6	119	10.0	10.0	119
Netherlands	1,635.2	1,635.2	231	3,227.9	3,227.9	8	1,592.7	1,592.7	21	1,641.4	1,641.4	21
New Caledonia	1.1	1.1	136	4.2	4.2	155	3.1	3.1	144	3.2	3.2	145
New Zealand	-88.3	-88.3	42	260.3	260.3	47	348.5	348.5	49	362.3	362.3	49
Nicaragua**	-125.3	-125.3	37	89.2	89.2	76	214.5	214.5	58	219.7	219.7	58
Niger	1.6	1.6	141	1.8	1.8	177	0.1	0.1	193	0.2	0.2	193
Nigeria	85.5	85.5	204	230.8	230.8	51	145.3	145.3	65	150.4	150.4	65
Niue	(-)	(-)	104	(-)	(-)	(X)	(-)	(-)	215	(-)	(-)	215
Norfolk Island	-1.1	-1.1	91	(-)	(-)	230	1.1	1.1	159	1.2	1.2	160
Norway	-37.1	-37.1	52	241.5	241.5	50	278.6	278.6	53	292.9	292.9	53
Oman*	-8.7	-8.7	70	117.7	117.7	71	126.3	126.3	66	135.3	135.3	66
Pakistan	-165.2	-165.2	34	131.4	131.4	68	296.5	296.5	52	312.1	312.1	52
Palau	1.8	1.8	142	1.8	1.8	176	(-)	(-)	222	(-)	(-)	222
Panama*	682.3	682.3	227	714.2	714.2	30	31.9	31.9	91	33.1	33.1	92
Papua New Guinea	31.9	31.9	191	38.5	38.5	96	6.5	6.5	125	6.7	6.7	126
Paraguay	148.8	148.8	216	166.4	166.4	59	17.7	17.7	106	19.0	19.0	107
Peru*	212.4	212.4	220	755.5	755.5	29	543.2	543.2	38	581.9	581.9	38
Philippines	-151.6	-151.6	35	689.9	689.9	32	841.5	841.5	31	870.6	870.6	31
Pitcairn Islands	(-)	(-)	106	(-)	(-)	231	(-)	(-)	221	(-)	(-)	221
Poland	-88.7	-88.7	41	299.9	299.9	45	388.6	388.6	44	403.3	403.3	44
Portugal	-85.5	-85.5	43	94.4	94.4	74	179.8	179.8	60	186.8	186.8	60
Qatar	-12.9	-12.9	64	145.7	145.7	62	158.6	158.6	64	162.7	162.7	64
Reunion	-1.8	-1.8	85	0.6	0.6	189	2.5	2.5	147	2.5	2.5	149
Romania	-96.5	-96.5	40	80.7	80.7	79	177.2	177.2	61	186.1	186.1	61
Russia	-925.6	-925.6	16	644.6	644.6	34	1,570.2	1,570.2	23	1,639.7	1,639.7	22
Rwanda	-5.1	-5.1	73	0.3	0.3	203	5.4	5.4	131	5.5	5.5	132
Samoa	3.0	3.0	152	3.2	3.2	158	0.2	0.2	191	0.2	0.2	191
San Marino	-0.4	-0.4	96	0.1	0.1	212	0.5	0.5	172	0.6	0.6	172
Sao Tome and Principe	(-)	(-)	111	(-)	(-)	222	(-)	(-)	208	(-)	(-)	208
Saudi Arabia	-627.9	-627.9	19	1,527.7	1,527.7	19	2,155.6	2,155.6	18	2,258.7	2,258.7	17
Senegal	26.1	26.1	190	27.9	27.9	104	1.8	1.8	150	1.9	1.9	150
Serbia	-37.2	-37.2	51	6.2	6.2	147	43.3	43.3	86	44.0	44.0	87
Seychelles	1.0	1.0	134	1.3	1.3	184	0.3	0.3	183	0.3	0.3	183
Sierra Leone	5.1	5.1	161	5.4	5.4	151	0.3	0.3	182	0.4	0.4	182
Singapore*	1,036.3	1,036.3	228	2,302.4	2,302.4	13	1,266.1	1,266.1	25	1,282.5	1,282.5	25
Sint Maarten	92.7	92.7	205	97.2	97.2	73	4.5	4.5	136	4.5	4.5	138
Slovakia	-61.1	-61.1	46	53.1	53.1	91	114.2	114.2	71	116.8	116.8	71
Slovenia	-18.2	-18.2	58	33.0	33.0	99	51.2	51.2	81	52.9	52.9	81
Solomon Islands	-1.2	-1.2	89	0.2	0.2	206	1.4	1.4	155	1.5	1.5	155
Somalia	4.6	4.6	158	4.7	4.7	154	0.1	0.1	200	0.1	0.1	200
South Africa	-243.4	-243.4	29	475.7	475.7	40	719.1	719.1	33	733.6	733.6	34
South Sudan	1.1	1.1	139	1.1	1.1	185	(-)	(-)	(X)	(-)	(-)	(X)
Spain	-127.4	-127.4	36	917.8	917.8	26	1,045.2	1,045.2	27	1,091.0	1,091.0	27
Sri Lanka	-239.6	-239.6	30	21.6	21.6	119	261.2	261.2	55	273.0	273.0	55
St Helena	-0.5	-0.5	94	0.1	0.1	218	0.5	0.5	173	0.5	0.5	174

Exhibit 4a. Exports, Imports, and Trade Balance of Goods by Country and Area, Not Seasonally Adjusted: 2015

In millions of dollars. Details may not equal totals due to rounding. (X) Not applicable. (-) Represents zero or less than one-half unit of measurement shown.

Country	Balance (Customs imports)			Exports Domestic & Foreign, F.A.S. basis			Imports Customs basis			Imports C.I.F. basis		
	January	Year-to-Date	Rank	January	Year-to-Date	Rank	January	Year-to-Date	Rank	January	Year-to-Date	Rank
St Kitts and Nevis	5.1	5.1	159	13.0	13.0	131	7.9	7.9	124	8.1	8.1	125
St Lucia	43.6	43.6	196	44.5	44.5	94	0.9	0.9	164	1.0	1.0	163
St Pierre and Miquelon	(-)	(-)	112	(-)	(-)	224	(-)	(-)	(X)	(-)	(-)	(X)
St Vincent and the Grenadines	3.9	3.9	154	3.9	3.9	156	(-)	(-)	205	(-)	(-)	206
Sudan	1.2	1.2	140	1.3	1.3	181	0.1	0.1	196	0.1	0.1	195
Suriname	4.5	4.5	157	32.2	32.2	100	27.7	27.7	95	29.7	29.7	93
Svalbard, Jan Mayen Island	(-)	(-)	(X)	(-)	(-)	(X)	(-)	(-)	(X)	(-)	(-)	(X)
Swaziland	1.1	1.1	138	1.5	1.5	180	0.4	0.4	179	0.4	0.4	179
Sweden	-418.5	-418.5	25	295.5	295.5	46	714.0	714.0	34	731.7	731.7	35
Switzerland	-467.2	-467.2	21	1,691.3	1,691.3	17	2,158.5	2,158.5	17	2,179.1	2,179.1	18
Syria	-0.4	-0.4	97	0.3	0.3	199	0.7	0.7	169	0.7	0.7	168
Taiwan	-1,191.9	-1,191.9	12	1,918.7	1,918.7	15	3,110.5	3,110.5	11	3,225.6	3,225.6	11
Tajikistan	0.6	0.6	131	0.6	0.6	193	(-)	(-)	216	(-)	(-)	216
Tanzania	-2.6	-2.6	82	11.3	11.3	133	13.9	13.9	111	14.1	14.1	111
Thailand	-1,153.6	-1,153.6	13	1,057.8	1,057.8	24	2,211.5	2,211.5	16	2,289.3	2,289.3	16
Timor-Leste	0.1	0.1	117	0.1	0.1	217	(-)	(-)	(X)	(-)	(-)	(X)
Togo	10.0	10.0	174	10.8	10.8	135	0.8	0.8	166	0.9	0.9	166
Tokelau	(-)	(-)	113	0.1	0.1	219	(-)	(-)	206	(-)	(-)	205
Tonga	0.8	0.8	133	1.1	1.1	186	0.3	0.3	187	0.3	0.3	184
Trinidad and Tobago	-349.0	-349.0	26	178.4	178.4	56	527.4	527.4	39	563.5	563.5	39
Tunisia	14.9	14.9	179	58.6	58.6	88	43.7	43.7	85	44.7	44.7	85
Turkey	226.4	226.4	221	900.0	900.0	27	673.6	673.6	36	710.9	710.9	36
Turkmenistan	8.2	8.2	172	8.8	8.8	142	0.6	0.6	170	0.7	0.7	170
Turks and Caicos Islands	24.9	24.9	188	25.2	25.2	113	0.3	0.3	184	0.3	0.3	185
Tuvalu	(-)	(-)	108	(-)	(-)	228	(-)	(-)	213	(-)	(-)	211
Uganda	-0.1	-0.1	100	5.9	5.9	148	6.0	6.0	128	6.2	6.2	130
Ukraine	23.2	23.2	187	89.6	89.6	75	66.4	66.4	77	71.1	71.1	77
United Arab Emirates	1,662.3	1,662.3	232	1,864.6	1,864.6	16	202.3	202.3	59	213.6	213.6	59
United Kingdom	251.8	251.8	223	4,423.3	4,423.3	5	4,171.6	4,171.6	7	4,255.4	4,255.4	7
Uruguay	94.7	94.7	206	140.4	140.4	65	45.7	45.7	83	47.1	47.1	83
Uzbekistan	15.4	15.4	181	16.5	16.5	124	1.2	1.2	157	1.3	1.3	158
Vanuatu	-0.2	-0.2	99	0.3	0.3	201	0.5	0.5	174	0.6	0.6	173
Vatican City	0.3	0.3	129	0.3	0.3	200	(-)	(-)	(X)	(-)	(-)	(X)
Venezuela	-885.3	-885.3	18	693.5	693.5	31	1,578.8	1,578.8	22	1,630.4	1,630.4	23
Vietnam	-2,165.3	-2,165.3	8	528.0	528.0	38	2,693.4	2,693.4	13	2,820.3	2,820.3	13
Wallis and Futuna	0.1	0.1	118	0.1	0.1	216	(-)	(-)	(X)	(-)	(-)	(X)
West Bank Administered by Israel	-0.9	-0.9	93	(-)	(-)	223	0.9	0.9	165	0.9	0.9	165
Western Sahara	(-)	(-)	105	(-)	(-)	229	(-)	(-)	214	(-)	(-)	214
Yemen	-15.3	-15.3	60	13.5	13.5	128	28.8	28.8	93	28.9	28.9	95
Zambia	-3.1	-3.1	79	8.1	8.1	144	11.2	11.2	117	11.4	11.4	116
Zimbabwe	-9.3	-9.3	69	2.5	2.5	167	11.8	11.8	114	11.9	11.9	115
Unidentified (1)	(-)	(-)	(X)	(-)	(-)	(X)	(-)	(-)	(X)	(-)	(-)	(X)

Exhibit 4a. Exports, Imports, and Trade Balance of Goods by Country and Area, Not Seasonally Adjusted: 2015

In millions of dollars. Details may not equal totals due to rounding. (X) Not applicable. (-) Represents zero or less than one-half unit of measurement shown.

Country	Balance (Customs imports)			Exports Domestic & Foreign, F.A.S. basis			Imports Customs basis			Imports C.I.F. basis		
	January	Year-to-Date	Rank	January	Year-to-Date	Rank	January	Year-to-Date	Rank	January	Year-to-Date	Rank
Africa	66.4	66.4	(X)	2,214.5	2,214.5	(X)	2,148.1	2,148.1	(X)	2,222.6	2,222.6	(X)
APEC	-46,599.6	-46,599.6	(X)	75,351.6	75,351.6	(X)	121,951.2	121,951.2	(X)	125,704.0	125,704.0	(X)
ASEAN	-5,325.5	-5,325.5	(X)	6,176.3	6,176.3	(X)	11,501.8	11,501.8	(X)	11,901.8	11,901.8	(X)
Asia - South	-2,924.8	-2,924.8	(X)	1,765.0	1,765.0	(X)	4,689.8	4,689.8	(X)	4,887.6	4,887.6	(X)
Asia Near East	-598.0	-598.0	(X)	5,535.5	5,535.5	(X)	6,133.6	6,133.6	(X)	6,349.0	6,349.0	(X)
CAFTA-DR	700.9	700.9	(X)	2,341.9	2,341.9	(X)	1,641.0	1,641.0	(X)	1,728.0	1,728.0	(X)
Central American Common Market	376.6	376.6	(X)	1,763.0	1,763.0	(X)	1,386.4	1,386.4	(X)	1,465.9	1,465.9	(X)
Euro Area	-8,029.5	-8,029.5	(X)	16,607.1	16,607.1	(X)	24,636.6	24,636.6	(X)	25,164.5	25,164.5	(X)
Europe	-10,434.3	-10,434.3	(X)	26,200.6	26,200.6	(X)	36,635.0	36,635.0	(X)	37,478.3	37,478.3	(X)
European Union	-9,323.1	-9,323.1	(X)	22,265.7	22,265.7	(X)	31,588.8	31,588.8	(X)	32,272.2	32,272.2	(X)
LAFTA	-2,811.4	-2,811.4	(X)	27,500.0	27,500.0	(X)	30,311.4	30,311.4	(X)	30,932.9	30,932.9	(X)
NATO Allies	-9,042.2	-9,042.2	(X)	43,934.2	43,934.2	(X)	52,976.4	52,976.4	(X)	54,249.6	54,249.6	(X)
NICs	-726.3	-726.3	(X)	10,402.7	10,402.7	(X)	11,129.0	11,129.0	(X)	11,495.8	11,495.8	(X)
North America	-5,859.5	-5,859.5	(X)	41,607.1	41,607.1	(X)	47,466.6	47,466.6	(X)	48,300.1	48,300.1	(X)
OECD	-23,175.6	-23,175.6	(X)	77,071.6	77,071.6	(X)	100,247.2	100,247.2	(X)	102,379.0	102,379.0	(X)
OPEC	-1,121.8	-1,121.8	(X)	5,613.9	5,613.9	(X)	6,735.7	6,735.7	(X)	7,016.3	7,016.3	(X)
Pacific Rim Countries	-36,878.4	-36,878.4	(X)	29,617.6	29,617.6	(X)	66,496.0	66,496.0	(X)	69,017.7	69,017.7	(X)
South/Central America	2,086.4	2,086.4	(X)	12,749.8	12,749.8	(X)	10,663.4	10,663.4	(X)	11,186.3	11,186.3	(X)
Twenty Latin American Republics	-1,367.8	-1,367.8	(X)	30,665.4	30,665.4	(X)	32,033.3	32,033.3	(X)	32,744.0	32,744.0	(X)

* Countries denoted by asterisks represent countries with Free Trade Agreements with the United States.
** Countries denoted by double asterisks represent countries included within Free Trade Agreements with the United States.

Africa - Algeria, Angola, Benin, Botswana, British Indian Ocean Territories, Burkina Faso, Burundi, Cameroon, Cape Verde, Central African Republic, Chad, Comoros, Congo (Brazzaville), Congo (Kinshasa), Cote d'Ivoire, Djibouti, Egypt, Equatorial Guinea, Eritrea, Ethiopia, French Southern and Antarctic Lands, Gabon, Gambia, Ghana, Guinea, Guinea-Bissau, Kenya, Lesotho, Liberia, Libya, Madagascar, Malawi, Mali, Mauritania, Mauritius, Mayotte, Morocco, Mozambique, Namibia, Niger, Nigeria, Reunion, Rwanda, Sao Tome and Principe, Senegal, Seychelles, Sierra Leone, Somalia, South Africa, South Sudan, St. Helena, Sudan, Swaziland, Tanzania, Togo, Tunisia, Uganda, Western Sahara, Zambia, Zimbabwe.

APEC (Asia - Pacific Economic Cooperation) - Australia, Brunei, Canada, Chile, China, Hong Kong, Indonesia, Japan, Korea (South), Malaysia, Mexico, New Zealand, Papua New Guinea, Peru, Philippines, Russia, Singapore, Taiwan, Thailand, Vietnam.

ASEAN (Association of Southeast Asian Nations) - Brunei, Burma, Cambodia, Indonesia, Laos, Malaysia, Philippines, Singapore, Thailand, Vietnam.

Asia - South - Afghanistan, Bangladesh, India, Nepal, Pakistan, Sri Lanka.

Asia Near East - Bahrain, Gaza Strip Administered by Israel, Iran, Iraq, Israel, Jordan, Kuwait, Lebanon, Oman, Qatar, Saudi Arabia, Syria, United Arab Emirates, West Bank Administered by Israel, Yemen.

CAFTA-DR (Dominican Republic-Central America-United States Free Trade Agreement) - Costa Rica, Dominican Republic, El Salvador, Guatemala, Honduras, Nicaragua.

Central American Common Market - Costa Rica, El Salvador, Guatemala, Honduras, Nicaragua.

Euro Area - Austria, Belgium, Cyprus, Estonia, Finland, France, Germany, Greece, Ireland, taly, Latvia, Luxembourg, Malta, Netherlands, Portugal, Slovakia, Slovenia, Spain.

Europe - Albania, Andorra, Armenia, Austria, Azerbaijan, Belarus, Belgium, Bosnia-Herzegovina, Bulgaria, Croatia, Cyprus, Czech Republic, Denmark, Estonia, Faroe Islands, Finland, France, Georgia, Germany, Gibraltar, Greece, Hungary, Iceland, Ireland, taly, Kazakhstan, Kosovo, Kyrgyzstan, Latvia, Liechtenstein, Lithuania, Luxembourg, Macedonia, Malta, Moldova, Monaco, Montenegro, Netherlands, Norway, Poland, Portugal, Romania, Russia, San Marino, Serbia, Slovakia, Slovenia, Spain, Svalbard, Jan Mayen Island, Sweden, Switzerland, Tajikistan, Turkey, Turkmenistan, Ukraine, United Kingdom, Uzbekistan, Vatican City.

European Union - Austria, Belgium, Bulgaria, Croatia, Cyprus, Czech Republic, Denmark, Estonia, Finland, France, Germany, Greece, Hungary, Ireland, taly, Latvia, Lithuania, Luxembourg, Malta, Netherlands, Poland, Portugal, Romania, Slovakia, Slovenia, Spain, Sweden, United Kingdom.

LAFTA (Latin American Free Trade Area) - Argentina, Bolivia, Brazil, Chile, Colombia, Ecuador, Mexico, Paraguay, Peru, Uruguay, Venezuela.

NATO (North Atlantic Treaty Organization) Allies - Belgium, Bulgaria, Canada, Czech Republic, Denmark, Estonia, France, Germany, Greece, Hungary, Iceland, Italy, Latvia, Lithuania, Luxembourg, Netherlands, Norway, Poland, Portugal, Romania, Slovakia, Slovenia, Spain, Turkey, United Kingdom.

NICs (Newly Industrialized Countries) - Hong Kong, Korea (South), Singapore, Taiwan.

North America - Canada, Mexico.

OECD (Organization for Economic Cooperation and Development) - Australia, Austria, Belgium, Canada, Chile, Czech Republic, Denmark, Estonia, Finland, France, Germany, Greece, Hungary, Iceland, Ireland, Israel, Italy, Japan, Korea (South), Luxembourg, Mexico, Netherlands, New Zealand, Norway, Poland, Portugal, Slovakia, Slovenia, Spain, Sweden, Switzerland, Turkey, United Kingdom.

OPEC (Organization of the Petroleum Exporting Countries) - Algeria, Angola, Ecuador, Iran, Iraq, Kuwait, Libya, Nigeria, Qatar, Saudi Arabia, United Arab Emirates, Venezuela.

Pacific Rim Countries - Australia, Brunei, China, Hong Kong, Indonesia, Japan, Korea (South), Macau, Malaysia, New Zealand, Papua New Guinea, Philippines, Singapore, Taiwan.

South/Central America - Anguilla, Antigua and Barbuda, Argentina, Aruba, Bahamas, Barbados, Belize, Bermuda, Bolivia, Brazil, British Virgin Islands, Cayman Islands, Chile, Colombia, Costa Rica, Cuba, Curacao, Dominica, Dominican Republic, Ecuador, El Salvador, Falkland Islands (Islas Malvinas), French Guiana, Grenada, Guadeloupe, Guatemala, Guyana, Haiti, Honduras, Jamaica, Martinique, Montserrat, Nicaragua, Panama, Paraguay, Peru, St. Kitts and Nevis, Sint Maarten, St. Lucia, St. Vincent and the Grenadines, Suriname, Trinidad and Tobago, Turks and Caicos Islands, Uruguay, Venezuela.

Twenty Latin American Republics - Argentina, Bolivia, Brazil, Chile, Colombia, Costa Rica, Cuba, Dominican Republic, Ecuador, El Salvador, Guatemala, Haiti, Honduras, Mexico, Nicaragua, Panama, Paraguay, Peru, Uruguay, Venezuela.

(1) The export totals reflect shipments of certain grains, oilseeds, and satellites that are not included in the country/area totals.

NOTE: Area data reflect the composition of the areas at yearend.

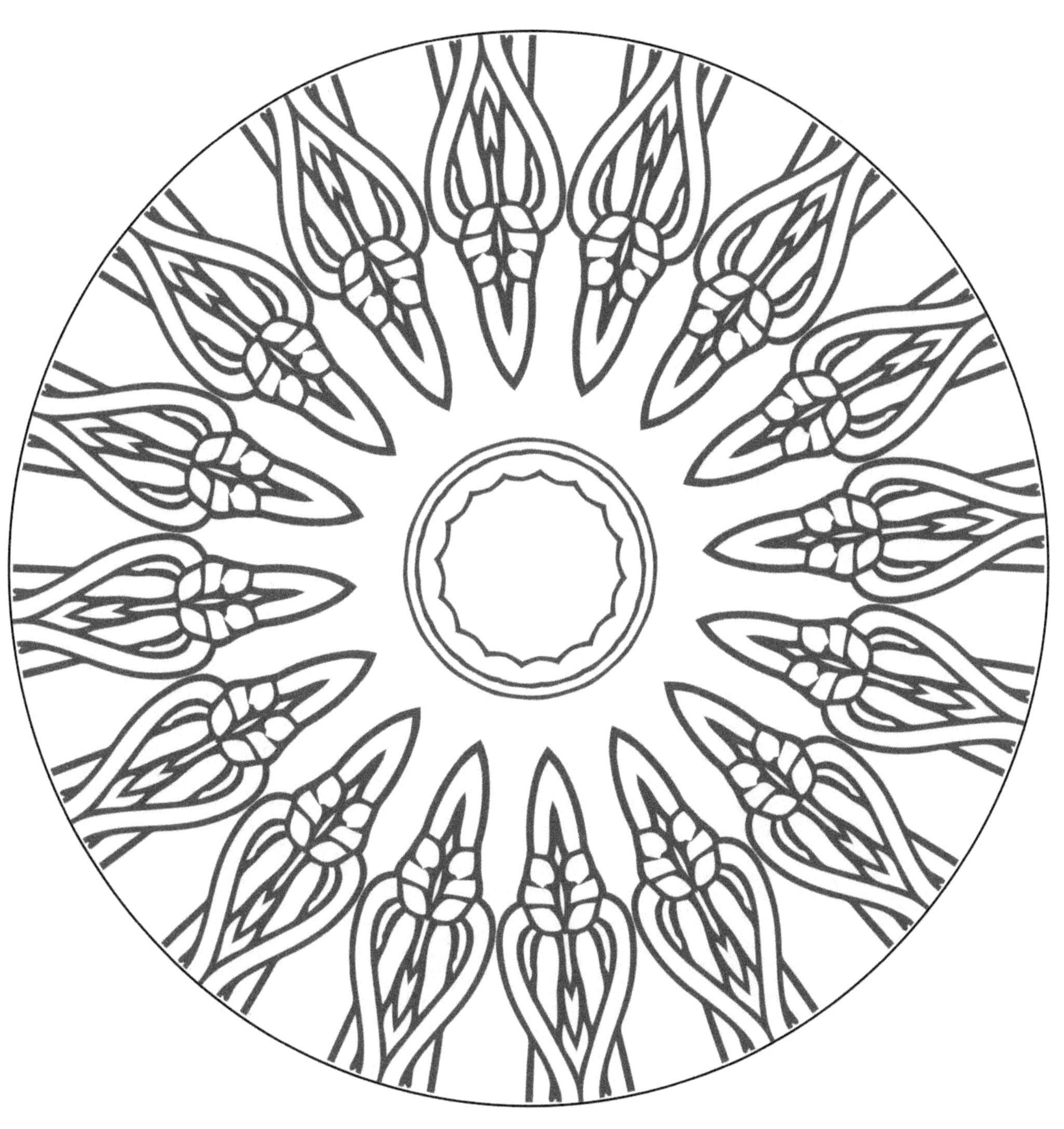

Please keep an eye out for new coloring books or visit stressfreecoloring.org for new options from me and info regarding other newly released coloring books!

If you enjoyed the coloring please let other color enthusiasts know by leaving a review ☺

Other Titles by Victoria Clarke

Yummy Treats – A Delicious Adult Coloring Book
25 Custom Illustrated Images of Treats

http://www.amazon.com/Yummy-Treats-Adult-Coloring-Book/dp/1532809301

Floral Motif Coloring Book
25 Custom Designed Floral Patterns

http://www.amazon.com/Floral-Motif-Relaxing-Pattern-Coloring/dp/1533077088

www.ingramcontent.com/pod-product-compliance
Lightning Source LLC
Chambersburg PA
CBHW080554190526
45169CB00007B/2771

* 9 7 8 1 5 3 3 2 4 4 3 8 3 *